But What Does _God_ Say About Me?

…discovering and embracing your true value

Janine Dodds

ISBN: 1-4107-7081-8 (e-book)
ISBN: 1-4107-7082-6 (Paperback)

Library of Congress Control Number: 2003094857

This book is printed on acid free paper.

Printed in the United States of America
Bloomington, IN

All Scripture quotations are taken from the New International Version unless otherwise indicated.

1stBooks – rev. 08/06/03

Table of Contents

Acknowledgements

To my spiritual father, Joseph Gonzales, better known as Papa Joe, whom the Lord used to start me on my journey of discovering my true value in Christ…Thank you for adopting me into your life, and for the hours, days and years you have invested into mine. How I love and appreciate you.

To my precious daughter, Tiffany…You are my "Sunshine". May you always see yourself through your Father's Eyes. I am so thankful that He chose me to be your mother and for giving me the privilege and joy of raising you. I love you so.

To my Heavenly Father…You are Almighty God, and yet you allow me to call you "Abba Daddy". Thank you for loving me before I ever loved You. Thank you for teaching me and lovingly revealing to me how You see me. Thank you also for your encouragement, guidance, and wisdom while writing this book. I am forever grateful. I love You and adore You!

TO GOD BE THE GLORY!

Beginning Your Journey

Our identity and how we view ourselves affects our lives on a daily basis in how we treat ourselves and how we treat others. It also has an effect on our achievements, our goals and our desires.

Much of our sense of our value is derived from what others have said to us and about us throughout our lives, starting in childhood and up to present day. No matter what others have said to us, it is necessary that we unlearn anything we have believed that is contrary to what God says about us...no matter how long we have believed it and no matter who taught us those beliefs. We must negate anything we have believed about ourselves that does not line up with God's Word, and then replace it with His Truth. We must *learn and believe* what our Heavenly Father says about us. The more we look to God for our identity, the less we will look to others for it and the less we will *need* to look to others for it. Peoples' opinions of us differ and are always subject to change. Therefore, if we look to others for our identity, we will constantly be confused. *But God's opinion* of us never changes nor does His Love for us. When He is the source of who we are, we can walk and live in security and confidence.

Many people use their achievements, who their parents are, who their spouse is, etc. as a basis for their self worth. But those things do not provide a solid foundation. Accomplishments can enhance our self esteem but when they become the root, we are walking on shaky ground. And attributing our sense of value to our relationship to another person does not always prove stable either. Once we know our true value *in Christ*, then our foundation is strong and our lives are enhanced. By having our value in Christ as our foundation, we are protected from the "winds of change" which are inevitable in life. If our sense of value is based upon what we do, who we are, what we own, our accomplishments, our abilities, our age, our looks, etc., all of these are subject to change. Therefore, when they do change and are not in our life anymore, then our sense of worth becomes shaky or nonexistent. On the contrary, when we know that our true value comes through who we are in Christ and His Love for us and how He sees us, then we are able to actually accomplish more in life. *But* our self esteem will not be rooted in those other *changeable* things…it will be established in our value to God…which is never changing. Because of our human weaknesses and frailties we need to look to God as our source of confidence and esteem.

So what does God say about this matter of how we view ourselves and its effect on how we treat others? Romans 12:2 says, "Do not conform any longer to the pattern of this world, but be transformed by the renewing of your mind..." By choosing to read this book and begin this journey, you have taken a step toward that. Congratulations! The benefits are well worth the effort.

People who are well established in their identity with the Lord can handle fame and acceptance as well as rejection and failure because they see themselves through God's Eyes and not the world's eyes. Becoming well known or popular will not throw them off the track to become arrogant or conceited. Nor will being disliked or rejected cause them to crumble. I'm not saying it doesn't hurt to be rejected. Of course it does. We are human and God gave us emotions. Being wanted and liked by others feels good, and being cast aside by people does hurt. But in life, we all experience both ends of that. The difference in how we deal with these feelings and the effect they have on us is based on our foundation. Do we see our worth through God's Eyes or through the eyes of others?

The more we come to see ourselves as God sees us, the more we are aware of and embrace our true identity in Him. And then the less we will be tossed about by the ever changing world around us, because we are anchored to Him. He *never* changes and His Love for us is everlasting.

3

Malachi 3:6 – "I, the Lord, do not change."

James 1:17 – "…Who does not change like shifting shadows."

Jeremiah 31:3 – "…I have loved you with an everlasting love…"

The title of this book begins with the word "but". This was done to make a very strong point. Anytime the word *but* is used, it automatically negates or casts doubt on or discredits or weakens whatever was said prior. More emphasis is always put on what comes *after* but. So things that have been or are being said to you, or things you have believed about yourself, should start causing you to think, "*But* what does **God** say about me?"

The purpose of this book is to help walk you through an examination of what has been said to you throughout your lifetime, and to see if what you have been believing about yourself lines up with what God says about you. If it does, then you are very blessed indeed. You have a true sense of your own value and how God sees you. If, on the other hand, what you have been believing does not line up with what God says, then I pray that this book will be a vehicle that He can use to help get you on the path of seeing yourself through His Eyes.

In opening this book you have taken a step on a most wonderful journey. *Take your time.* Give yourself plenty of space to absorb and digest what God is speaking to your heart as you walk through these pages. Some steps along the way may bring to your mind someone whose words helped build you and strengthen you because they valued you as God does. Rejoice and thank the Lord for that person(s)! My mother was such a person to me. Although she died when I was only 19, the positive effects of her edification of me have lasted throughout my lifetime. Another was my 4th grade teacher, Wesley William Roberts, Jr.

As you continue on this journey, you may come upon some steps which may be slightly tender or even very painful. But don't be afraid to walk there. You are *not* alone. God will be with you every step of the way. He loves you so...

His Delight in You

Have you ever watched new parents standing over their baby? If you have children, you can remember those feelings. Each little sound, or facial expression, or move is noticed. Each whimper or cry is examined and tended to. The skin texture is so soft it calls out to be touched. The hair so fine it feels like silk through our fingers. The head and face, feet and hands are just made for caressing and kissing.

Have you also noticed how a person's demeanor changes around a baby? Their voice gets higher, their face comes alive and they lean into/over the baby. There's just something about a new baby that causes us to delight in them.

Well, multiply that delight a few thousand times and it still won't come close to God's delight in you. And while the awe and wonder of a new baby and everything it does tends to lessen a bit with time, that is *not* true for God's delight in us. He gets the same joy and takes the same delight in His children, whether they are a few minutes old or 85 years of age. It never changes.

Even if your parents don't have a lot of baby pictures of you or they don't share a lot of happy stories with you, or in some cases, your birth and infancy (for some reason *you* had no control over) was not a happy time for them...it *was* a time of joy for your Heavenly Parent.

He took great delight in you *and still does.* He rejoiced over you with singing *and still does.* (Zephaniah 3:17) And His photo album!!! He has snapshots of His children for every day of their lives. When you won the Spelling Bee, He said, "That's My girl!" When you ran your fastest and still came in last in the race, He said, "That's My boy!" Those times you blocked traffic in order to rescue a turtle crossing the road...He appreciated you watching over His creatures. And when you stood up to the bully who was picking on a smaller child...He saw that. The time you were the only one who showed up to do the elderly woman's yardwork...and then you took extra time to visit with her when she brought you lemonade. Yes, He saw that, too. And that time you stopped for a traffic accident and stood in the rain to comfort a total stranger who was frightened...He was there. Remember all those times when you did special things for others and nobody even knew you were the one? God knew. And He took great delight in you, His child.

He *still* does.

Your Importance to Him

God must think it's important for us to know how valuable we are to Him...He threaded this message throughout the old and new testaments. We are so important to God! We matter to Him! He values us! You may think, "Why do I matter when God has billions of people to care about? Surely a few slip through the cracks...why should I think I'm important to Him?" Well, let's look at what God says about us. Isaiah 49:16 says, "See, I have engraved you on the palms of My Hands..." Think about that. Almighty God has you engraved on the palms of His Hands!

Have you ever seen someone write a note to themselves on their palm? Why did they write it *there*? Because it would be easily seen all the time! You are engraved on God's Palms! Not just your name...but YOU...your face, your thoughts, all the things that are part of you. Isn't that exciting to know? You know how you feel when you see your picture on someone's refrigerator or in their home or even in their wallet? You feel important to them. It shows that they want a reminder of you in their presence. Well, the same is true of our importance to our Father, but so much more so.

People can move into and out of our lives and pictures can be taken down or even discarded. *But* God cannot "unengrave" you from His Hand. Better yet, He doesn't want to. Just knowing that should make you feel like you are the most important person in the world! And you are, you know. Each of us is. Acts 10:34 tells us, "...I now realize how true it is that God does not show favoritism..." This means He has the same love for each one of us. No person is more important to Him than any other. So, if He loves us all the same, then how can He make each and every one of us feel like the most important person to Him? Because He's God.

David prayed in Psalm 17:8 for God to keep him as the "apple of His Eye". In Matthew 10:29-31 Jesus tells us that a sparrow falling to the ground does not go unnoticed by Him. He tells us that we are worth more than many sparrows. He even knows how many hairs are on our head! This should show us how significant we are to Him and that He cares about the details of our lives.

Some of you reading this remember the pain in childhood of not being chosen when teams were being picked or perhaps being the last one chosen. Perhaps you were not asked to join a particular club.

Even as an adult, it can hurt when we're bypassed for a promotion or left off an invitation list or neglected at some gathering.

But do you know what *God* says about you? He says in John 15 that *He chose you* out of this world. He chose you and appointed you to go and bear fruit for Him. How awesome it is when we get a true grasp of that revelation! Almighty God, Heavenly Father, Maker of Heaven and Earth, the Alpha and Omega, Ever Present, All Knowing and All Powerful God...

CHOSE YOU.

Psalm 139

The first 16 verses of this Psalm represent the ultimate in healthy self esteem. It reads like a love letter from God to us. Because of the lengthy detail that God put into this particular segment of Scripture, I decided that it deserves a chapter of its own in this book.

Make yourself comfortable, get a cup of coffee or tea, clear your mind of distractions and get ready to be loved on by your Father...

v.1 – "O Lord, You have searched me and you know me."

No one knows us like God does...He knows us thoroughly and intimately.

v.2-4 – "You know when I sit and when I rise; You perceive my thoughts from afar. You discern my going out and my lying down;

You are familiar with all my ways. Before a word is on my tongue You know it completely, O Lord."

God knows every move we make, every thought we have, and every word we say before we even say it. *And* He still loves us deeply and unconditionally!

v.5 – "You hem me in behind and before; You have laid Your Hand upon me."

God is constantly with us and keeps His Hand upon us…just as a parent keeps a hand on a small child.

v.6 – "Such knowledge is too wonderful for me, too lofty for me to attain."

We cannot understand these things about God because His Ways are so much higher than ours. We must simply accept His Love by faith…in our spirits. Our human minds are just not capable of comprehending God.

v. 7-12 – "Where can I go from your Spirit? Where can I flee from your presence? If I go up to the heavens, You are there; if I make my bed in the depths, You are there. If I rise on the wings of the dawn, if I settle on the far side of the sea, even there Your Hand will guide me, Your right Hand will hold me fast. If I say, "Surely the darkness will hide me and the light become night around me," even the darkness will not be dark to you; the night will shine like the day, for darkness is as light to You."

There is nowhere we can go where God is not with us. And wherever we are, He is guiding us and holding on to us tightly. If you have a wayward child or spouse or loved one, you can take comfort in this passage.

v.13-15 – "For You created my inmost being; You knit me together in my mother's womb. I praise You because I am fearfully and wonderfully made; Your works are wonderful, I know that full well. My frame was not hidden from You when I was made in the secret place. When I was woven together in the depths of the earth, Your Eyes saw my unformed body."

God created you…listen to that. Almighty God created *you.* Of all the uplifting verses in the Bible showing my value to God, these touch my heart the most. Just think…before your mother even knew of your presence in her womb, your Father was knitting you together…and doing it in such a unique fashion that He made your fingerprints, your ears, your voice like *no other person*…past, present or future! And for nine months He continued to weave your precious little body together perfectly while still making you unique…one of a kind. He never took His eyes or His Hands off of you. Oh, how this revelation blesses me!

v.16 – "All the days ordained for me were written in your book before one of them came to be."

God was and is aware of every event in each day of your life and He's always known of these things *before* they have ever happened. Some of you may be thinking that if God knows about everything in our lives ahead of time, then why doesn't He prevent the bad things from happening? The answer is simple. He gives us free will. Some choose to exercise that freedom by following God, loving Him and others, and living their lives according to God's principles. Others, however, choose not to. We also have a formidable enemy (satan) whose purpose is to draw people away from God and to do things his way. Because of mankind's free will, many people get hurt.

You must realize, though, that God is a *good God* and He is Love. He is NOT the author of rape or incest or adultery or fornication. Some of you reading this were conceived in those circumstances. Or perhaps you've been told that you were "unplanned" or "unwanted". It is *vital* that you understand that no matter what conditions you were conceived in, you were still created by God. Even if the conception conditions were not in God's will, *you* still are very much His will and He has always had a plan for your life because you are special, unique, and very precious in His sight!

Let that truth penetrate your heart and sink deep into it. If you have ever believed that you are somehow "damaged goods" or "inferior" due to the circumstances surrounding your conception, you need to acknowledge *that belief* right now, and forever, for what it is...a LIE. The same holds true for your birth experience and your childhood. These are things you had no control over. So why would you believe that an all knowing, loving God would hold you responsible for or label you for things you could not control or change. He *doesn't*...nor should you.

Think, for a moment, about the care you put into something you created...a painting, or some other form of artistic expression, a dress you made, a house you built, a special meal you prepared, a poem or book you wrote, a craft you designed, etc. The list goes on. The point is that you know what it feels like to "create" something. You've experienced the planning, the excitement, the joy and pride in seeing it come to be...of seeing your creation unfold before your eyes. Well, take all your feelings and thoughts and multiply them by the grains of sand on the earth and it still won't equal the joy and love and excitement that God felt when He was creating...*you.*

Think on that!

God's Availability and Faithfulness

True friends are a blessing. They add to and enrich our lives in so many ways. God blesses those relationships now the same as He did in Biblical days such as with David and Jonathan's friendship.

We've all experienced friends who have not been faithful to us, for one reason or another, or have disappointed us. Jesus certainly knows what that feels like. His closest friends fell asleep when He needed them the most (Matthew 26). And His most vocal friend denied even knowing Him when the pressure was on. (Matthew 26). Paul also had friends who deserted him or betrayed him. (2 Timothy 4)

The opposite is true as well. None of us has been a totally available or totally faithful friend. Either way, when this happens, the pain can run deep. Sometimes this is caused by selfishness or laziness or jealousy or other things that we humans fall prey to. Reconciliation is always a possibility. God is a God of restoration.

But communication by *both* parties is crucial and reconciliation must be desired by both, as well.

Sometimes it may be God's will that the relationship not continue but I don't believe it's ever His will that it end with bitterness or misunderstanding, both of which are satan's playground. Without two-way communication, that could very well be the result.

You may have different friends who God has placed in your life for different purposes. One friend may challenge you in your growth. Another may be one who always makes you laugh. Another has great compassion and can provide comfort to you when needed. Perhaps another has wisdom and experience and God uses that one to teach you. He also puts particular friends in our lives because there are things within us that they need. Friends brought together by God are truly a gift to one another!

What do we do, though, when one of those friends is not available when we need them? Have you ever had a time when you really needed to talk and called several friends and *not one* was available? I have, and the potential for panic or fear is present. But neither panic nor fear is God's will. It is during a time like that that He speaks to us softly and tenderly and says, "I am here. You've called everyone else but Me." "Call on Me and I will answer you." (Jeremiah 33:3)

Wow! Talk about a revelation. So many times when we need someone or something, we run all about seeking that *one* who can help, while overlooking the *One* who is truly the source of our help.

Imagine being with someone who has a problem and *you* have the answer and you're standing right beside them. You're even wearing a "name tag" that says, "I Am the Way." But they are jumping all about looking around you, over you, everywhere but *to* you. How would you feel? As humans, we might want to just walk away, while thinking, "I have the solution to their problem and they are choosing to look everywhere else and ignore me. I'm wasting my time here." Well, thank God He doesn't react as we might. He remains by our side and waits for us to turn to Him. Oh, how patient and loving He is!

I believe that it is in those times that He is reminding us that yes, He blesses us with good friends and He uses them to speak to us and help us. But they are still only human and they have limits and their availability has limits and their loyalty can fluctuate as well as their feelings. Also, as much as a friend truly *desires* to help, sometimes they just do not have the ability to do what is needed. *God* is the only Friend Who is without limits of *any* kind.

Let's talk about that Friend Who is always available…24/7…and is always faithful to us and always communicates with us. And this friendship is most definitely for a lifetime…and beyond. That Friend is Jesus Christ. He is the only One Who is able to be all of the above and so much more.

Regarding availability, He has that covered. His phone number is Jeremiah 33:3, "Call to me and I will answer you…" He is always there, no busy signals, no answer machines, no annoying call waiting.

Psalm 120:1 says, "I call on the Lord in my distress and He answers me."

Psalm 145:18 states, "The Lord is near to all who call on Him…"

And faithfulness? He's cornered the market on that, too.

Psalm 145:13 – "…the Lord is faithful to *all* His promises and loving toward *all* He has made."(italics mine)

What about ability? Wow! That's a chapter in itself! God has the desire *and* the ability *and* the power *and* the authority to help you.

Daniel 3:17 – "…the God we serve is able to save us…"

Ephesians 3:20 – "Now to Him Who is able to do immeasurably more than all we ask or imagine…"

2 Timothy 1:12 – "…I know Whom I have believed and am convinced that He is able…"

Hebrews 7:25 – "…He is able to save completely those who come to God through Him…"

Jude 24 – "To Him who is able…"

Don't worry about Him disappointing you. Isaiah 49:23 assures us, "…and all those who hope in Me will not be disappointed."

Who can make these kinds of promises and actually has the ability *and* the desire to keep them?

Only God

One last note…There are times in our lives when God purposely has us walk through "wilderness times"…times of quietness and solitude, when God draws us away from others. These times can be quite lonely, humanly speaking. If we're not leaning on our Father, it's easy to misunderstand His purpose and to actually resent that time. Please don't make that mistake. For it is during those times alone with Him, that He is doing a work in you. He is preparing you for something great and He is always with you.

Notice in the Scriptures that before God used people for mighty things, He often had them experience wilderness times. Moses, David, Joseph, Elijah, John the Baptist, Paul…all went through a period of solitude before God used them mightily. Even Jesus spent 40 days in the desert before beginning His earthly ministry.

If you are going through a time like this now, I urge you to see this period as an opportunity and a blessing…that Your Father has carved out a chunk of time just for you and Him. Embrace that time. It really is an honor. I'm not going to say it always feels like a blessing, because loneliness can be painful. But trust that if God has placed you on this path for now, then that's the best place for you to be and that He is right there with you. Also remember that it is a preparation time and that it will come to an end…and waiting for you will be something wonderful that God has planned for you to do!

He Never Leaves You

Have you ever wished that you had someone in your life that you could truly count on to always be there…I mean *always?* Well, you do. Jesus is that Someone. Proverbs 18:24 states, "…there is a friend who sticks closer than a brother."

Perhaps your spouse left you, or a parent left you or died when you were a child, or you are in your golden years of life and your grown children have forsaken you or neglect you. Maybe you lived in different foster homes as a child and were never secure about where home was. These scenarios are played out all the time between people. The result is that many people are familiar with the pain of abandonment.

God is the *only* One Who promises He will never leave you nor forsake you (Hebrews 13:5) and actually keeps the promise.

In Psalm 139, He makes it very clear with many examples that no matter where you go, that He is with you. Not only is He with you, but in Psalm 32:10, He says that His Love *surrounds* those who trust in Him. Imagine that! He is not just by your side...He is surrounding you!

When Jesus ascended, His last Words to His disciples were, "I am with you always." (Matthew 28:20). You may be thinking, "But He said He'd always be with us and yet He left." He is no longer with us in bodily form, but He is very much with us in the form of the Holy Spirit. He told the disciples that He had to go but that He was leaving the Holy Spirit with them. He made it clear so that we would know we had not been forsaken, and that He would truly always be with us.

When a mother has to leave a young child for a while, she brings in a baby sitter. This way the child is never left alone. But even though the child is not alone, a sitter is still not the same as "Mommy".

When Jesus left the earth, He left Someone much better than a sitter for us so we wouldn't be alone. He left *Himself* in the form of the Holy Spirit. In doing so, He was saying, "I have to leave for a while but I will still be with you." How amazing!

How is this possible? He is God, that's how.

His Plans for You

Have you ever wondered why you were put on this earth? What purpose is there for you being here? Some of you may have been told that you were a mistake or that you will never amount to anything. Perhaps you heard the cruel words, "I wish you'd never been born." If so, I am so very sorry for the pain those words caused you. Chances are, you might have taken a different path in life had you heard different words. Chances are, you would have reached higher, accomplished more, and treated yourself and others differently had you heard different words.

But this is a new day. It's never too late to make changes. Let's see what God says about His plans for you. In Jeremiah 29:11 He says, "...for I know the plans I have for you, declares the Lord, plans to prosper you and not to harm you, plans to give you hope and a future." Make sure you hear that...prosper you, not harm you, hope, a future. This is wonderful news! In Jeremiah 31:17, He says again that there is hope for your future. Jeremiah 32:40-41 states that He will never stop doing good to us and He will rejoice in doing good to us. Wow!

Before Jesus ascended, He told us what His plans were for us. We were to continue on with the work He began during His 3 year ministry on earth. This is outlined in Matthew 28 and Mark 16. He also said we were to do *greater* things (in His Power) than He had done! (John 14:12) Imagine that!

So does God think you amount to something? Most definitely! Does God have wonderful plans for you? He sure does! Is God glad you were born and do you fit into His Plans?

Listen closely now...

OH, YES!!!

His Comfort & Compassion

The world says "laugh and the world laughs with you. Cry and you cry alone." That is just so sad. *But God says,*

Psalm 34:18 - "He is close to the brokenhearted…"

Psalm 145:18-19 - "The Lord is near to all who call on Him…He hears their cry and saves them."

Psalm 147:3 – "He heals the brokenhearted and binds up their wounds."

Psalm 145:14 – "The Lord upholds all those who fall and lifts up all who are bowed down."

Psalm 145:8 – "The Lord is gracious and compassionate…"

Psalm 116:5 – "…our God is full of compassion."

Does this sound like you are alone? No way. When you hurt, God hurts. There is a difference in sympathy and empathy. Many people are capable of feeling sympathy. But God truly feels and understands our pain. He walked this earth for 33 years in the form of Jesus Christ and He experienced physical, emotional, and spiritual pain at such depth that we will never know. He knows pain and He knows *our* pain. More important, He cares and He is there for us…always.

Have you ever had a "fair weather friend"? Most of us have. They're around for the good times but when a dark cloud appears on the horizon, they disappear. God isn't like that and He wants us to know that He cares about our hurts…so much that He threaded this message throughout His Word. One book of the Bible, which seems to have a concentration of this message is the book of Psalms. That is why so many people throughout the ages have turned to it for comfort. It is a book of prayer and praise. Of the 150 Psalms, David wrote about half. God called David "a man after My Own Heart". Wait a minute, didn't David commit some pretty terrible acts? He sure did…we have, too. And although he had to suffer the consequences of his mistakes, God was still there to comfort him and even protect him while he was being unduly chased and hunted by Saul, a maniac in a position of power. David cried out to God for literal help and protection, and God answered him.

I'm so thankful that all of David's story is told in the Bible...not just his strengths and victories and good qualities. Why? Because David was human...like us...and made some poor choices...like us...and was comforted by his God...like us. If you are not familiar with David's life, it would be so helpful for you to study him. It would help give you a picture of how God sees you and your value to Him. You can find his story in 1st and 2nd Samuel.

A while back I went through the most painful event of my life. It was totally unexpected, to say the least. I felt like I had been broadsided by a freight train. Granted, I've been through some rough things prior to that. But this particular situation cut so deep into me that I didn't know if I wanted to survive it. Have you ever had your heart broken that way? When the pain is so intense that there aren't even words to describe it? I know that many of you reading this can identify.

Although people were involved in this situation, I knew who was behind it...my one and only enemy...satan. His purpose is to steal, kill, and destroy. (John 10:10). He would have been quite pleased if I had turned away from God in my pain and then blamed God for what happened.

satan knows our achilles heels and he will go after them with a vengeance, if his other methods haven't worked. This particular attack was just that. He attacked the one area in my life where he knew he could do the most damage. He is evil and cruel and proud of it. His message to me was, "You're not going to make it through this time."

But the One Who lives in me is greater and more powerful than my enemy. (1 John 4:4) In my agony, I ran into His Arms and collapsed there…for months. As long as I needed His comfort and strength, it was there for me. He used people to comfort and support me, as well, to pray with me and for me, but God was still the source of it all. I knew that if I clung to Him that I would make it.

I spent a few days at the beach during this time and it was there that God ministered His indescribable comfort to me in such a special way. It certainly wasn't the only time. There have been many. But it's one of those times when He touches us in such a way that it makes a permanent impression on our hearts. I did a lot of walking on the beach during that visit and there were times when His presence next to me was so strong that it was as if I should have been able to see His footprints in the sand along with mine! Perhaps the one set of prints I did see *were* His…He was "carrying me" during that time. If you are familiar with the poem "Footprints in the Sand", you will understand.

Anyway, I knew that I knew that I knew I was not alone! He was holding me tight for as long as I needed Him to. During that same week, God spoke to me through His Word in such a powerful way. I was sitting on the beach reading in the Psalms. The Lord directed me to Psalm 94:18-19 which reads, "When I said, "My foot is slipping", Your Love, O Lord, supported me. When anxiety was great within me, your consolation brought joy to my soul." When I read those verses, they came to life, leapt off the page and landed in my heart.

I thought I had used up all my tears but as I set there meditating on those Words, feeling the warmth of the sun on my face and the Touch of the Son on my shoulder, the tears flowed. But these tears weren't filled with pain like the others. They were full of thanksgiving…for what had happened regarding the circumstances? No. But for God's comfort and compassion. For knowing that my Father cared and loved me and wasn't going to let me "crash on the rocks below". I sat there and read those Words…those Words of love and comfort from God to me, over and over and over again, until I knew them by heart.

Did my situation change immediately? No, it didn't. *But,* I knew for sure that my Heavenly Father…my Daddy…was with me…generously giving me what I so desperately needed…comfort. And I knew that I was not alone in this.

Oh, how I long for each and every one of you reading this to *know* God's comfort when you are hurting. Even more so, *He* longs for you to know Him that way. The next time you are hurting, whether it's the darkest part of night or early in the morning or the middle of the day…reach out…you will find His Hands already there reaching out for you.

You are not alone.

God's Forgiveness

Have you ever heard someone say something like, "I will never forgive you for that." Or perhaps, "I can never forgive him for what he did." On the other side of the same coin is, "I'll never forgive myself for doing that." Whether unforgiveness is directed at others or ourselves, it is dangerous territory and it is not what God says He wants for us.

There is a very good reason that He continually emphasizes the importance and necessity of forgiveness throughout His Word. He knows the damage it causes us when we allow unforgiveness to reside in us or when we refuse to accept His forgiveness. We are negatively affected emotionally, spiritually, and even physically. Simply put, there is just no good that comes of unforgiveness.

People who harbor unforgiveness are seldom joyful, peaceful, giving individuals. They may manage to rise to the occasion when necessary, but if you scratch deep enough on their surface, you will see the telltale signs of unforgiveness. Bitterness, anger, meanness, lack of compassion…these are all fruit of the tree of unforgiveness in a person's heart. It's an ugly crop, isn't it?

Physically, an unforgiving person can experience poor health because the effects of unforgiveness are literally eating away at them. When our minds are not at peace or are not *at ease*, it can manifest physically as "dis-ease". Our bodies were not designed to be in a constant state of stress and still remain healthy. Unforgiveness causes stress and after a while our bodies can break down as a result.

God says He desires that we prosper and be in health, even as our soul prospers. (3John 2) Our soul is our mind (our thoughts, emotions and desires) and He is showing a connection between our health and our thinking.

The most important and lasting aspect of forgiveness and unforgiveness is their spiritual ramifications. The very foundation of Christianity is that God sent His Son, Jesus, to shed His blood and die so that *our* sins could be forgiven. Then we could be restored to right relationship with God, the Father. Without the shedding of Jesus' precious blood, there could be no possibility for us to spend eternity with Him or to have fellowship with Him in this life.

So, being that forgiveness is the cornerstone of our faith, it is simply not an option for us to receive it or to give it. It is mandatory. I can almost hear the groans and see some of you squirming right about now…ouch…but please read on because, as the author of this book, I can tell you, "I've been there!" But when I was first told that I must forgive something that had happened to me, I didn't just groan or squirm. I flatly and firmly declared, "I can't do that!" in a tone of voice that said, "How dare you expect that of me after what has happened!"

I need to insert here that I was not a Christian at the time. A dear Christian lady I had met about a year prior to this incident had been praying for me all that time, without my knowledge. I knew there was something special and "different" about her and I felt somehow that she cared. So, when this thing happened, who did I call? You guessed it. After all, I reasoned that she was one of those "religious" people who had a special connection with God.

I did not realize it at the time but even though God did not orchestrate the incident that happened, He was most certainly using it for my good and for His glory. Oh, isn't hindsight wonderful!

Anyway, my anger over the situation had escalated within a couple of hours to such a point that it frightened me. So, I called this lady and she was home and available to talk. (Isn't it neat that when God sets up a divine appointment, He takes care of all the details?) Needless to say, I was not calm, but she was, and remained that way. After I told her what had happened and how upset I was, I ended by saying, "Please pray for me, okay? Bye."

I was about to hang up when she finally spoke. She hadn't had much of a chance before that. She said, "Yes, I'll pray for you, but I want to pray *with* you, too." God had control of this conversation, for sure. It was His Peace that overpowered the forces of evil that wanted me to get off the phone right then. God's Peace is a mighty weapon against the enemy! I sensed something in her voice and agreed to let her pray with me on the phone. At one point in the subsequent conversation, she said that I needed to forgive this individual. Oh boy, I didn't want to hear that. (This is what I meant earlier about hearing your groans). She was using God's wisdom and when I stated strongly, "What? I can't do that." She responded with words I have never forgotten. "I know you can't." I promptly jumped on that with "Then why are you saying I need to?" She then said, "On your own, you can't, *but* with the Lord, you can." Wise words, powerful words, life changing words. I replied with, "How do I do that?"

At this point, the angels were poised because they knew a celebration in Heaven was about to take place. (John 15:10) Before we hung up, I had given my life to Jesus Christ and asked Him to be my Savior. Thus began my journey with Him. I had received His forgiveness and then was able to forgive the individual who had hurt me. (Ephesians 4:32 and Colossians 3:13)

I shared this part of my testimony because it was the need for forgiveness, both to receive and to give, that brought me to the Lord.

If I had chosen to not forgive, the only "winner" in the situation would have been satan. he delights in unforgiveness.

If you ever have any doubt about whether or not you should forgive someone, or wonder if what they did to you is just too big for you to forgive, think about this. God has chosen to forgive you for everything you ever did wrong...not just the "minor violations". He doesn't have a scale that He uses to determine which sins or acts are forgivable and which are not. Jesus paid the price...His shed blood...for *all* of them. That truth will always bring things into perspective.

Another reason to keep your slate clean is because in Matthew 6:14-15, Jesus says that if we forgive others then God will forgive us. Then He adds, that if we do *not* forgive others, then God will *not* forgive us. Wow! That is serious business and not something to be overlooked or gambled with.

Initially, when you are struggling to forgive someone, this Scripture alone should be enough motivation to cause you to do the right thing. I can remember times when I had been hurt deeply and really didn't want to forgive. I preferred to focus on the verse about vengeance is mine, says the Lord. And that verse *is* true but it does not eliminate our responsibility as God's children to forgive. I had to accept that I needed God's forgiveness regularly too much. And *nothing* done to me is bigger than my need for His forgiveness.

It's important to point out that when we forgive someone for a wrong they have done, it does *not* mean we are excusing or condoning their behavior. Not at all. It also does *not* mean that we are to trust them right away. (When trust is broken or damaged, it takes time and effort for it to be restored.) Forgiving a person just means we choose to not harbor ill feelings toward them regarding what happened. It does not mean they are free of the consequences of their actions. But we are not to seek revenge…even if they are not sorry for what they did. God says that vengeance is His and that He will repay. (Deuteronomy 32:35 and Romans 12:19) It is not for us to do. God is aware of every injustice and He will deal with it. And He doesn't need us to counsel Him on how and when to handle it, either.

Another important note is that in the case of certain types of injuries someone has caused to you, it would be unwise and unsafe to allow that person into your heart or your home, or even be near them. Sometimes we are injured by people who have absolutely no remorse for their actions, and there is a strong possibility that they will repeat the offenses. You still have to forgive them *but* you do not have to be around them or allow them to be a part of your life. Do not allow the enemy to make you think you have not forgiven them. God does not expect us to put ourselves at risk or in danger in order to *prove* that we have forgiven someone.

Also, when you choose to forgive someone, please understand that you are doing this out of obedience to God and that the "feelings" of forgiveness may not automatically accompany the decision to forgive. Don't worry about that. God honors our obedience and He will bring our emotions in line with our decision, in time. I have had times when I've said to God through clenched teeth that I'm forgiving someone out of obedience and faith that God will bring my feelings in line. He always has. As I said, He honors obedience and He honors faith.

Be careful not to allow satan to convince you that you have not forgiven someone just because you still don't *feel* like you have. He does the same thing to Christians regarding their salvation. He will make them doubt if they are saved because at times they may not *feel* saved, even though they know they are. Don't get drawn into a debate with him. Just tell him immediately that he is a liar, and go on about your business. He does not deserve the time of day...don't give any of yours to him. Go by what you *know*, not by what you feel. Emotions are wonderful and God gave them to us so that our lives would have flavor and spice. But they are not always the best barometer simply because they can change so quickly and easily.

Now what about when we are the one who has caused an injury to another? It is just as important to acknowledge to ourselves and to that person what we've done and to ask them for forgiveness. Their response is not our responsibility. That must be left in God's Hands. But it *is* our duty to make certain that we truly have remorse over what we did and that our apology is sincere, and that it is also accompanied by any necessary recompense. Beyond that, you cannot control the situation. You are free of any guilt over it or any need to continue apologizing and asking for forgiveness. The other person's decision to forgive you or not to forgive you is between them and God.

There is one last point I want to make in this chapter and it is very important. We must realize and accept that once we ask God's forgiveness about something we have done, then it is a closed issue in His Eyes. Unlike asking forgiveness of a person, with God it is *always* granted! Hallelujah! A person may say, "I'll forgive but I won't forget." As humans, we can't just "forget" all of our injuries. But when someone makes a statement like this, it is usually an indication that they haven't forgiven.

With God, though, it's different. He truly does forget our sins and mistakes once we ask for forgiveness of Him. In Jeremiah 31:34, He says that He will remember our sins no more. In Psalm 103:12, He tells us that He has moved our transgressions from us as far as the east is from the west. He also states in Micah 7:19 that He puts our forgiven sins in the depths of the sea. Long ago, I heard someone say that God puts up a sign by this sea that says "No Fishing". In other words, once we ask for forgiveness from God regarding something we've done, He grants it and it is done...finished. He puts it into the sea of forgetfulness. We are not to bring that incident up to Him again.

If you are having nagging thoughts about it and feeling guilty, God isn't doing that to you. Guilt doesn't come from Him. Conviction? Yes. Guilt? No. Also the conviction comes *before* you ask forgiveness, not *after*. Remind yourself that you have asked forgiveness, you have settled any needed recompense, and that you stand forgiven. Amen.

In closing, I would like to say that if anyone ever tells you that you don't deserve to be forgiven for something you've done, you need to know that that is *not* what God says about you. Let these words from the Scriptures sink deep into your heart and mind.

Acts 10:43 – "...everyone who believes in Him receives forgiveness of sins through His Name."

Jeremiah 33:8 – "I will cleanse them from all the sin they have committed against me and will forgive all their sins of rebellion against me."

Psalm 130:4 – "But with You there is forgiveness..."

Colossians 1:14 – "...in Whom we have redemption, the forgiveness of sins."

Proverbs 28:13 – "...whoever confesses and renounces his sins finds mercy."

And here's a real gem, which will refute any thoughts or words such as, "God may have forgiven you, but He's still mad at you."

Nehemiah 9:17 – "…But you are a forgiving God, gracious and compassionate, slow to anger and abounding in love…"

That's what God has to say about it.

Choose to believe Him!

Your Righteousness

Did you know that you are righteous? Yes, you. If you are a child of God, then you have righteous standing before Him. You may be thinking, "Well, that's just impossible." You are correct if you mean righteousness on your own merit. We can never achieve right standing before God in and of ourselves…no matter how good we act or try to be.

Our righteousness comes through Jesus Christ and the sacrifice He made on our behalf. He took on our sin…all of it, past, present and future…and gave us His righteousness. 2 Corinthians 5:21 – "God made Him Who had no sin to be sin for us, so that *in Him* we might become the righteousness of God." (italics mine)

This is known as the "great exchange". What a deal *we* got! Not so for Him. But He did so willingly because without that exchange we would not be able to have a relationship with the Father.

For a deeper understanding of this, please read 2 Corinthians 2:11-21. This explains about the ministry of reconciliation.

After we become a Christian, God sees us as "justified"…just as if I'd never sinned. Our spirits have been made clean and new. When He looks at us, He does not see all the faults and blemishes, etc. He sees us as righteous before Him. That righteousness comes through being "washed" in the blood of the Lamb…Jesus Christ. I like to think of it this way…God has "before" photos of each of us. And they are *not* a pretty sight! Once we become His child, He then takes an "after" photo which is beautiful! (Now keep in mind that these photos are *not* of our physical bodies or our minds. These photos are of our spirits.) The good news is He throws away the before photos! Isn't that wonderful? He never again sees us spiritually as we were before coming to Him.

And you know what? We shouldn't either. The only reason we should ever take a peek at that old photo or think about it is to remind ourselves and testify to others about what God has done for us and how good He is. But we are not to dwell on or allow others, especially satan, to keep bringing out that old photo. 2 Corinthians 5:17 tells us, "Therefore, if anyone is *in Christ*, he is a new creation; the old has gone, the new has come!" (italics mine)

As far as our *mind* is concerned, we have to renew it and that is a lifelong process. Romans 12:2 says, "Do not conform any longer to the pattern of this world, but be transformed by the renewing of your mind..." How do we do that? By spending time with the Lord, spending time in His Word, worshipping Him, praying, and learning from and fellowshipping with other Christians. You don't have to struggle and strain to renew your mind. If you just are *willing* and desiring for God to help you and mold you, then He will. He loves a teachable person. Just like a teacher loves a student who wants to learn, and will do almost anything to help those who are *willing.*

An important point here...If you're thinking "Now, I'm God's child but I have all this work to do to renew my mind. I'm weary just thinking about it!" First, God loves you just the way you are! He also loves you too much to let you stay that way. So, does renewing your mind make God think more highly of you or love you more? Absolutely NOT! God will never love you more than He already does. And that does not change! But He knows that for *your* good, there are some areas in your life (and nobody is exempt here) that need to be changed so that you will be able to enjoy a full and rich life. The things He desires to see changed are actually things that are holding you back from living your life to the fullest. Once we get to heaven, these things will not matter because it is our spirits that go to heaven, not our minds. But as long as we live on earth, we have to deal with our minds, which encompass our thoughts and emotions.

So, don't think you have to make changes in order to please God. He sees you (your spirit) as righteous before Him through

Christ. The reason He wants us to renew our minds is because it affects the way we treat ourselves and others. What kind of witness is it if we say we are Christians and then live our lives and conduct ourselves just like the world? One of our responsibilities as God's children is to bring others into His Kingdom. One way we do that is by our actions. And our behavior is affected by our thoughts, which are in our mind. I'm sure you can see where I'm going with this. When we renew our mind, cleansing it of the "impurities" it contains, then our behavior and attitudes become more like our spirit...more Christlike. Our spirit, which is already like Jesus, can then show through and others can see it. This is how many people come to know the Lord...by watching someone who loves Him and desires to live their life for Him. Jesus told us to share our faith with others so that they may come to know Him, too. There are many ways to do this...one, of which, is how we live our lives. To live a *perfect* life is not what God expects of us and it is unattainable. But because we have Christ living in us and therefore, have His Power in us, we can certainly strive toward excellence in all we do. A renewed mind will certainly put us farther ahead on that path.

Regarding your righteousness *in Christ*...if you are a child of God, then your righteousness is a fact. Whether you believe it or not, it remains true. God wants you to believe it and to see yourself that way. He wants you to approach Him knowing who you are in Christ and acting accordingly when you come before Him.

Do you expect or desire for your children to come crawling to you like worms every time they need something or want to talk with you or spend time with you? I don't think so. Do you want your young children to have to ask you every day if it's okay for them to live with you? Or to sit at your table to eat? Of course not. You want them to have the assurance and confidence of knowing that they are your children and that they belong with you and are welcome.

Well, it's the same with our Father. He doesn't want us begging for His attention and crawling up to Him with our heads bowed in shame as if we are some stranger who came in off the street begging for a handout. No. In Hebrews 4:16 we are told, "Let us then approach the throne of grace with *confidence*, so that we may receive mercy and find grace to help us in our time of need." (italics mine) With confidence we are to approach our God. That confidence comes from knowing we are righteous in His eyes because we have come to Him through the blood of the Lamb.

He wants us to come to the throne boldly, not timidly. Many people have a picture in their minds of God's throne being something like the wizard of Oz. Dorothy and her companions approached him shaking and trembling, feeling totally unworthy of his time, and filled with terror. The poor cowardly lion even jumped out of the window in fright. Well, this is not how our Father wants us to come to Him.

It's also important to point out that we are not to approach Him in such a casual manner as if to say, "Hey, Pops, I'm here." No way! He is our Father, for sure, *but* He is also **God.** We are to approach His Throne with respect and reverence and awe. He is God first and then He is our Father. It's important that we keep that in the proper order. We are to always respect His position as the Almighty God, Who also happens to be our Father.

Having said that, remember what the Scripture says about coming to the throne with confidence. Let's say you have an account at a bank and have money in that account. When you need to make a withdrawal from it, you go to the bank and ask for it. The first thing they will want to see is some identification to prove that you are who you say you are and that you have legal access to that account. Once you show some ID, then your withdrawal is processed. That's it.

Can you imagine anyone, after showing their ID, standing there and begging to make a withdrawal? Or crawling to the teller and pleading for money? Or after the withdrawal is processed and is handed to them, they refuse to accept it? They say something like, "I know the money is in my account because I put it there but I just don't feel worthy of accepting any." This would be ludicrous.

When we, as God's children, approach Him with timidity and fear (the unhealthy kind), we are basically doing the same thing. Apart from Christ, we have absolutely no right to go to God and ask for anything. Our name is not on the "account". (not written in the Lambs Book of Life – Revelation 21:27) *But* once our name *is* on the "account", we receive a "passWord" and that's *all* we need in order to approach. What is the passWord? Jesus Christ.

When we go to God about something…a need, guidance, comfort, a confession, or best of all just to say "Hi, Father, I love You."…we can walk into His Presence with Jesus by our side and know that before we say a word, Jesus has called ahead and said to God, "It's okay, Father, (s)he's with Me."

If you are "with Him", then approach God with confidence…knowing that you have right standing before Him, in Christ…knowing that you are welcome and wanted and loved.

Confidence vs Arrogance

We've all met people or know of someone who comes across as cocky or "full of themselves". We also see people who walk in a state of confidence that is admirable. They both seem sure of themselves so what is the difference? The *source* of their attitude and strength is what makes the difference. What power source are they connected to?

In John 15:5, Jesus says that apart from Him, we can do nothing. Then in Philippians 4:13 we are told that we can do everything through Him Who gives us strength. It is clear that our power source is to be the Lord, and not ourselves. When a person is arrogant, they are looking to themselves for strength. "Self" is *not* a reliable or lasting source and those who plug into self, at some point, discover that the well has run dry.

Jeremiah 17:4 & 7 reads, "This is what the Lord says: Cursed is the one who trusts in man, who depends on flesh for his strength and whose heart turns away from the Lord. But blessed is the man who trusts in the Lord, whose confidence is in Him." God makes it very clear which power source He wants us to be connected to. In that same chapter of Jeremiah, He details the consequences of each choice.

Confidence comes in knowing who we are *in Christ* and knowing *Whose* we are. Have you ever heard little children bragging about their fathers? "My father is stronger than your father." "My father is the smartest person in the world." "My father built our house." "My father can do anything!" These little ones have a sense of importance and value because of *who they belong to*. How much more should we, as children of Almighty God, have our sense of confidence based on Who we belong to! We can *truly* exclaim, "My Father is stronger and smarter and bigger than anyone!" "My Father built the world." "Nothing is too difficult for my Father." (Jeremiah 32:17)

The confidence we possess when we truly grasp the meaning of who we are *in Christ* enables and empowers us to do things far beyond our own ability level. Proverbs 28:1 says, "...the righteous are as bold as a lion." Psalm 138:3 reads, "...you made me bold and stouthearted."

When we are aware of our true identity, we gain victory in circumstances where the odds are stacked very high against us. Why? Because God blesses our faith in Him and in His Power and Wisdom. He blesses our dependence upon Him instead of on ourselves. When we acknowledge and embrace our dependence upon Him, He teams up with us in our efforts and gives us the victory! God plus one is a majority! Hallelujah!

An excellent example of this is found in 1 Samuel 17. David was just a small, young shepherd boy with a slingshot. Goliath was over 9 feet tall, was an experienced fighter, was carrying a javelin, a sword, and a spear, and was wearing armor that weighed around two hundred pounds. Who *should* have won this fight easily? Goliath, of course. But who came forth triumphant? David did. Why? Because in the natural, this was absolutely no match. But David wasn't operating in the natural, that is, in his own strength. His courage and boldness came from His faith in his God.

David was not a fool. He knew he was no match for this giant *on his own.* But he believed that he had been appointed for this task and he had already experienced victory through God in the past when he killed a lion and also a bear because they were attacking his sheep. His confidence was not in his own ability. His confidence was in His Lord! God did use David's ability with a sling, but it was David's *availability* that God blessed.

Goliath's taunts and intimidation went on for 40 days. No one stepped forward. They were afraid. And then when David did, he was accused by his older brother, Eliab, of being conceited. Eliab also insulted David's work as a shepherd...first by implying that being a shepherd was menial and unimportant. He then added on more insult by saying he only watched a "few" sheep. I don't know how many sheep David took care of but that is not the point. Eliab was saying this to insult him. How foolish of him! It was while tending those sheep that David learned how to use a sling...his weapon of choice against Goliath. It was also while tending those sheep that David received inspiration to write many of the Psalms. It was also while tending those sheep that David developed an intimate, deep relationship with God that would sustain him throughout his life and also give him the honorable title by God of "A Man after My Own Heart".

A note here before I continue...don't ever allow anyone to denigrate your work, if what you are doing is where God has put you at that time. It makes no difference if you are running a company, changing diapers and chasing toddlers full time, taking care of a sick or elderly person alone, or speaking before many people. God can and does use us where He places us and He can and does speak to us where He places us. And earlier when I said "anyone", that includes yourself. No matter what we are doing, we are to do our work as unto the Lord...just like David, the shepherd boy.

Now, back to the story. Eliab did not offer a solution to the problem and on top of that, he then had the audacity to insult and falsely accuse David when David stepped forward. If I had been there, I would have wanted to slap Eliab. Oops... "flesh flash"...sorry. But, as usual, God came through for David because he was doing what God had called him and empowered him to do. God and David became a majority.

When David charged toward Goliath, he was *shouting,* "I come against you in the Name of the Lord Almighty!" He was absolutely filled with confidence! In himself? No. In his ability with a sling? No. He was filled with confidence and faith in His God. He also knew he was not charging at that giant alone. God was *in* him and God was *with* him. Therefore, victory was assured. Hallelujah!

Why did David have five stones in his pouch? Was he thinking that in case his first shot missed, he would have 4 more chances? Hardly. The Scripture says David "ran quickly" toward the battle line to meet Goliath. That wouldn't leave much time to "reload". No, David knew that the first shot had to count and had to be the knock-out punch. But Goliath had brothers. David was so full of confidence in this victory, that, if necessary, he would take them out, too!

It's hard to imagine that a person running full speed can hurl a stone from a sling and have it hit a target as small as a man's forehead. This is where God comes in. When we obey Him and place our confidence in His Ability, then He will intervene when necessary to insure the victory or success. If David's aim had been the slightest bit "off", don't you think that God would have straightened its path? I do. His aim is perfect and He never misses. Praise God!

Goliath was killed and his army defeated because he was arrogant and had placed all his confidence in himself. He and his powerful army became the minority. David had victory because he was confident in His Lord and therefore, he and God became the majority.

I have a plaque on my kitchen wall that reads "The will of God will never lead you where the grace of God cannot keep you." God lead David into that confrontation...not to be humiliated or destroyed...but to have the victory. God's grace is sufficient for anything He leads us into. His grace is powerful and mighty!

Beware of "Eliabs" in your life. The original is gone but there are still plenty like him out there. When you are walking in the confidence of God, others can sometimes misunderstand and accuse you falsely of being arrogant or even foolish. You cannot listen to those voices. If you *know* for certain that you are doing what God has called you to do, then you must stand firm in that. To others, David probably did look arrogant and foolish. But if David had listened to

Eliab, he probably would have become full of doubt and fear…neither of which is from God. He then would not have done what God had prepared him for and called him to do. He also would have missed out on all the blessings and rewards of that victory.

I have taken bold steps of faith many times in my life. And there have been times when I have received criticism or skepticism from a few Christians as a result. It did hurt to hear their words of doubt but I believed that God had directed my steps and I stood my ground. To others, my actions may have looked foolish, but I can tell you this. God has always honored my position of faith and I give Him praise for that! He gave me a Scripture long ago, which has given me strength and encouragement many times. Isaiah 7:9 – "…If you do not stand firm in your faith, you will not stand at all." Someone told me long ago, not to expect everyone to agree or support you in all your decisions of faith, because God did not give *your* dream (idea, plan, desire, goal, direction, etc.) to *others*. He gave it to *you.* It is so nice, though, when you do have those who will agree with you in prayer and stand with you as you step out in faith to do what you believe God has called you to do.

Keep company with those believers who will encourage you in your faith. If they are not around, then you just have to do what David did. The Scripture says, "…but David encouraged himself in the Lord His God." (1 Samuel 30:6 KJV) Stand firm in your faith. God will bless you for it. Remember, a great oak tree is just an acorn that held its ground. If David had not held his ground when he was a little shepherd boy, and stood firm in his faith in God, this might have been the last we ever heard about him. Way to go, David!

Arrogance comes from an attempt to inflate "self". Humanism is based on worship of self. Whenever self is at the center, then God is not in it and He despises it. (Proverbs 16:5) He makes it very clear throughout Scripture that he hates pride...the kind of pride that lifts one up in an attempt to be equal to or above God. The first commandment He gave Moses was, "You shall have no other gods before Me." (Exodus 20:3) This includes the god of self. Lucifer, one of the archangels was kicked out of Heaven because of the sin of pride. he was determined that he would be equal to God and the result was that he was evicted and given a new name...satan. One of the meanings of his name is "deceiver". It fits. And the first person he deceived was him "self". Galations 6:3 – "If anyone thinks he is something when he is nothing, he deceives himself."

God hates all sin but the one that he judges most severely is pride. Proverbs 8:13 tells us, "...I hate pride and arrogance..." Some have misunderstood the word "pride" and believed that they should not be proud of their children, or their work, or even their own accomplishments. To be proud of someone or something is not the same as the pride spoken of earlier. It is good when we take pride in what we do and have an attitude of excellence. That is not the same as exalting yourself above God. We are to do our best while still giving the credit and glory to the Lord.

An arrogant person is usually trying to cover up something like an inadequacy, weakness, or insecurity of some type. We all have them. Without Christ we either cover them with a veil of arrogance and conceit or we portray ourselves as totally insecure.

But if we know who we are in Christ, then we can allow Him access to those areas. Then our weaknesses actually make us strong. In 2 Corinthians 12:10 Paul says, "...when I am weak, then I am strong." Earlier in that chapter, Jesus told Paul, "My grace is sufficient for you, for My power is made perfect in weakness." I know this sounds strange. God's Ways are not the same as man's ways...His ways are higher. God doesn't want us covering up our weaknesses and inadequacies and insecurities with arrogance. He wants us to yield them to His Grace and Power. He then, as a result, makes us strong. Our strength and confidence come from and through *Him*.

Think for a moment of a person in terms of layers. If you start peeling off the layers of an arrogant person, you will soon see that what is underneath is a frightened little boy or an insecure little girl. If, on the other hand, you peel off the layers of a confident individual who knows who they are in Christ and knows their value, you will find God at the core. Any "self" you find in those layers is being crucified daily. (1Corinthians 15:31) Paul writes in Galatians 2:20, "I have been crucified with Christ and I no longer live, but Christ lives in me..." This means that we are to have less self and more God in us. The more we allow God to be in us, the more strength we draw from Him and the less our weaknesses show. Our confidence grows and others cannot help but see that in us.

A word of caution. As our confidence level grows and we accomplish more, and enjoy more victories it can be easy to be tempted by the "prince of pride". When we hear a lot of things like "Wow, look what you've done!", it's important and a good safeguard to always reply with something like, "Thank you, look what God did through me!" or "Thank you, I did it *with God's help.*" This way you will not come across as "sickeningly" humble and unable to even accept a compliment, but you will be giving God the glory while you acknowledge your part in it.

God wants His children to be confident and successful. Just like we, as parents, want the same for our children. It takes a very ungrateful and arrogant child to attribute his success to his own ability and give none of the credit to his parents. Hmmm. When we experience success through our confidence in Christ and then fail to acknowledge Him as the source of that confidence and success...well, aren't you glad God doesn't have "flesh flashes"?

Even still, those who flirt with pride are treading in dangerous territory. Proverbs 16:18 says, "Pride goes before destruction, a haughty spirit before a fall." Wow…talk about a warning label! Any time we put our trust in ourselves and in our own abilities, we are playing with pride. Pride is a hungry, ravenous thing. It always wants more of you. If you don't recognize it right away for what it is, it can consume you. If you don't believe me, then just ask Lucifer…uh, I mean satan. But, of course, you can't believe a word he says so the safest and smartest thing to do is to believe what *God* says about it.

Just so that those who feel that they have been prideful or arrogant don't get the idea that God is mad at them or that they are about to be consumed with it…I want to say this. The very fact that you are concerned about that or examining yourself and your motives is a very good sign that you don't have a problem with pride. Usually, those who are eaten up with pride don't even realize it. If confronted, they will most likely deny it. Just as some alcoholics deny they have a drinking problem, an arrogant person will deny they have a pride problem.

God, in His Mercy, gives His children so many opportunities to correct this and humble *themselves* before Him. He is so patient with us. But He does have a limit as to how far He will allow someone to continue on that thorny path. Keep in mind that He hates pride. James 4:6 – "…God opposes the proud but gives grace to the humble." When we push Him to that limit, He then must humble us or allow our circumstances to humble us. He cannot and will not allow pride to continue in His children. Daniel 4:37 – "...and those who walk in pride He is able to humble." It is far better to wake up and humble ourselves before Him, rather than continue on and have to endure the alternative.

Another benefit of humbling ourselves before God is that He promises to exalt us. James 4:10 – "Humble yourselves before the Lord, and He will lift you up." And Matthew 23:12 – "Whoever exalts himself will be humbled, and whoever humbles himself will be exalted." Self-exaltation is a stench in His nostrils. Remember, that trait is what caused Lucifer to receive his "pink slip".

God wants us to exalt Him and to humble ourselves. The wonderful benefit is that *He* will exalt us! Since His Ways and His Thoughts are so much higher than ours (Isaiah 55:9) it makes sense to follow His instructions...and then reap the rewards.

I'd like to close this chapter on a lighter, positive note. Earlier on, I mentioned the good kind of pride. Christians, more than anyone, have a reason to be proud of who they are. (Hebrews 10:35-36) We are not supposed to walk around with our heads down, looking sad and defeated and unworthy. We are children of a king...*The* King, which makes us princes and princesses. Therefore, as children of the King, we have the best reason to walk tall and proud and feel good about who we are and Whose we are. There is no greater source of confidence than that!

Joy

Joy. It is listed as one of the fruit of the Spirit in Galatians 5:22. So God must think it's important that we have it. But how many of us do? When you look around at people, do you see joy in their countenance? Do they see it in yours? I truly hope so.

Being happy on the outside due to circumstances is not synonymous with joy (inner happiness unrelated to circumstances). Yes, happiness can be a by product of joy and the gift of being able to get excited over even little things can be a by product of joy. But these experiences are based on emotion and circumstances...both of which change constantly. True joy in our spirits is not an emotion. It is a state of mind or a way of life. It is embedded in our hearts. It does not waver. It remains steady no matter how the wind blows or how the waves come in. Paul says in Philippians 4:12, "...I have learned the secret of being content in any and every situation...I can do everything through Him Who gives me strength." Content is another way of saying happy.

Am I saying that we should feel joy when bad things happen? No. But the joy we have in our hearts because the Lord dwells there gives us the strength to face the difficult and painful things in life. The joy of the Lord is our strength. (Nehemiah 8:10) This does not mean we walk around constantly with huge smiles on our faces, or that we laugh in the face of pain or heartache. It means that no matter what happens, we have the strength to endure it because we have in our hearts the joy of knowing Jesus Christ personally and knowing all the benefits of that relationship. We also know that whatever is happening is temporal – it won't last – it's temporary – it will pass. But our relationship with God is eternal and the life we have ahead of us with Him is eternal. When our main focus is on those things, then we tend to not get as bogged down or knocked about by things that happen that are unpleasant or just plain bad. We know that at the end of this journey, (which God says is like a vapor), as God's children, we have something awaiting us that is too glorious and wonderful for words.

So does our time on earth really matter? Oh, yes! Jesus came so that we would have an abundant life. (John 10:10) He wants us to have good lives and to enjoy our lives. One of the ways we can enjoy our lives is through laughter. God mentions laughter many times in

His Word. I'm not talking about forced, artificial or superficial laughter. I mean real, from the belly, body shaking laughter!

When I think of what Jesus looks like I don't see Him as He is portrayed in so many paintings...as sad, somber and serious. I see Him lively, handsome, strong, with a great sense of humor and a big smile on His Face. My favorite depiction of Him is the one entitled the "laughing Jesus". In it, He is shown with His Head thrown back and His Mouth open with laughter! Oh, how I look forward to seeing Him Face to face and hearing Him laugh!

When I see someone who says they love the Lord and are living for Him and yet their countenance is so sour and bitter, it is sad. I cannot believe that God wants us, as His ambassadors, to be that way. We all have different personalities but sour and bitter is not a personality type...it is a choice. And we can also choose to have joy in our hearts, which will show on our faces. (Proverbs 15:13)

In Proverbs 17:22 it says, "A cheerful heart is good medicine, but a crushed spirit dries up the bones." This was written thousands of years ago. Science now acknowledges that laughter helps tremendously in keeping us healthy. When we laugh, a chemical is released in our body, which has healing properties. It actually affects our physical health! No wonder God said it was as "medicine". I read recently where a doctor said that laughter was one of the best ways to prevent cancer. How about that! Talk about a powerful prescription.

And we all know how good it feels emotionally when we enjoy a good laugh.

I have always laughed easily and a lot. I thank God for that! I also am thankful that I enjoy excellent health. I have come through many hard times and painful experiences and still have never "lost my laugh". There have been times when it seemed to be hidden for a while, but it always resurfaced. Perhaps it was all the years of laughter that was "stored up", and that inventory saw me through the lean times. God Himself created laughter and put it in us. Can you just imagine what life would be like without it? I don't even want to try.

Perhaps you've heard the saying that "most people are about as happy as they make up their minds to be." Laughter is a gift from God that He gives to *everyone.* It's our choice whether or not to receive that gift.

One of the ways I take care of myself is that I make sure that I have around me things that will make me smile and laugh. Sometimes it's people, certain photos, sometimes a movie, re-runs of the Andy Griffith Show or The Honeymooners always guarantee a good laugh! I have dolphins displayed in my home. I love dolphins because they are friendly, intelligent, love to play, always have a smile on their face, and have the cutest laugh.

As an animal lover, I have always had pets. I even smuggled a hamster into my dorm room in college. (Smuggling my dog in would have been a bit more challenging.) I have 3 dogs and the interaction between them, as well as with me, is so entertaining. You animal lovers reading this will understand what I mean when I call them "angels with fur". I know from experience that God uses animals to minister to us, not just through laughter, but through comfort and companionship as well. As I'm writing this, one of my pups just stood up in front of me with a silly look on her face, and then laid back down. Of course, I laughed. How timely. Sometimes I wonder just how much they understand!

I love the Smoky Mountains and visit there frequently. There is a place there called the Comedy Barn, which I have been to several times and I plan to go back. The staff, who also own the place, is dedicated to providing good, clean entertainment and they do an excellent job. It is 2 hours of non stop laughter. Being among several hundred people who are laughing so much is wonderful! I can almost envision Jesus sitting right there in the middle of it all having a great time.

Laughter can even be recycled. All you have to do is recall something funny and you get to enjoy it all over again and again and again. Isn't that neat how one seed of laughter can produce a harvest many times over?

It's important to note that not all laughter is of God or is good. When people laugh at someone's misfortune or make fun of someone, there is nothing funny about it. It's just plain cruel. Any laughter that causes pain for another is not coming from God. If you've ever been victim to something like that, then you know that kind of pain.

Jesus certainly knows. They laughed at Him and mocked Him during His horrible time on the cross and also before that. You can bet satan and his crew were laughing and having a grand ole time now that this Jesus was out of the way. *But*, their party and evil laughter only lasted 3 days! Hallelujah! And from that time on, we, as His believers, have had the last laugh.

But our laugh is not one of evil delight, it is one of pure joy because our Savior is risen indeed! And our joy and laughter will last much longer than 3 days...it will last an eternity! Glory to our Risen King!

If you have trouble laughing, then make a decision right now to "find your laugh" again. Every day, choose to look at, listen to, read about, and think about things that are funny. They are all around us if we will just make the effort to look. Laughter is contagious and is always amplified when shared. Share yours with others and with God. He will bless you with better health and a better appearance.

Philippians 4:4 says, "Rejoice in the Lord *always*. I will say it again: Rejoice!" (italics mine) Anytime something is repeated in the

Bible, it is for emphasis. Rejoice means to be full of joy and laughter. We need to celebrate and rejoice over our good circumstances, for sure! But when our circumstances, at times, aren't so good, we are told to still rejoice…

Rejoice in the Lord

Rejoice in the fact that He loves us

Rejoice that we will be with Him always

Celebrate the fact that He is risen

and we are free!

Hallelujah!

Peace

When you think about peace, perhaps you envision a world without war, a family with no arguing, a house that is quiet, or a day without problems. Well, you might experience days without fires to extinguish. Your house may be a quiet place. But as long as families are comprised of imperfect human beings, there will always be some disagreement. And peace in the middle east? Not likely. The problems there stem all the way back to Abraham and Sarah deciding to "help" God bring His Will to pass.

But there is a peace that we can have which is not based on circumstances such as those mentioned above. The kind of peace I am referring to is inner peace, which comes only from God. In John 14:27 Jesus tells us, "Peace I leave with you; my peace I give to you. I do not give to you as the world gives. Do not let your hearts be troubled and do not be afraid." This kind of peace has nothing to do with current events, the news, the weather, where we live, our social status, who our family members are, etc. On the contrary, God's peace can be maintained in our hearts and minds even if everything around us is crazy, upside down, or falling apart.

One of the greatest examples of this kind of peace is seeing someone remain calm in the midst of chaos and confusion. The peace of the Lord dwelling *in* them is more powerful than the circumstances *around* them. It doesn't mean that they are oblivious to what's going on, or are denying it. It does mean that they are not allowing those happenings to rob them of their peace.

Jesus, the Prince of Peace, *slept* in the boat while a storm was raging all around. He was then accused by His disciples, of not caring. Those who walk in this kind of peace are sometimes misunderstood. God's peace is not easy to understand if you have never experienced it. I hope that by the time you finish this chapter, you will realize that peace is something God definitely wants you to have.

Peace is *not the absence* of war or problems. Peace is the *presence* of God. Isaiah 26:3 reads, "You will keep in perfect peace him whose mind is steadfast, because he trusts in You." To "keep" means to protect, guard, and defend. This is a verse I repeat regularly, because it reminds me to look to Him always and to trust Him always. Easier said than done, huh? But the idea is that the more we focus on the Lord, the more He is magnified in our minds. Also the smaller and less threatening everything else around us appears.

Notice that there is a condition to Him keeping us in perfect peace. That condition being that we keep our thoughts on Him and His goodness and greatness and that we trust Him. We cannot run around frantically focusing on the problems and circumstances and constantly speaking of them, and then say, "Where is God's peace? God said He would keep me in peace!" God is not a liar and He *will* keep us in perfect peace if we do our part by placing our trust in Him.

None of us go through this life without stormy times. There is a song that I dearly love which talks about this. The song says that sometimes God calms the storm. (We are always so thankful when He does!) Other times, He allows the storm to continue on for a while or even rage around us. It is during those times that He wants to calm *us,* His children. The only way He can do that is if we stay close to Him, cling to Him, remain in His Arms where our safety is assured. When we are putting our energy and thoughts into Him and His protection and wisdom, then our mind isn't going crazy looking at what is going on around us.

When we comfort a child who is afraid, we draw them close and usually they bury their face in our chest or neck. We hold them tight in our arms and this reassures them that they are safe there. Imagine trying to comfort a child if he is running from you, frantically screaming about the storm and telling you how upset he is! Well, this is probably how *our* Father feels when we don't run to Him.

We need to just bury our face in His chest and allow His Peace to envelop us. Then when we look around, the storm will either be over or it will look less threatening to us. If we do have to endure it, we know that He will walk through it with us.

God also wants us to walk in His Peace because He knows that we will enjoy better health as a result. Proverbs 14:30 tells us, "A heart at peace gives life to the body..." Our bodies are made to produce a substance called adrenaline. God designed us this way for our protection. It was designed to be used in "flight or fight" situations...physical encounters which necessitate a surge of energy which enables us to run away from danger or stay and fight. It's also used in physical competition such as sports. When we feel threatened, our body automatically releases adrenaline to prepare us to fight or flee. Our body does not recognize whether the threat is physical or mental. It just senses a threat and releases adrenaline. This chemical creates a "high" in us as it empowers us. It enables us to do something beyond our normal physical capacity. But it was not designed for use on a regular basis or for everyday activities.

Unfortunately, though, like any "drug", people can become addicted to that "high" it provides. They want it more and feel that they cannot go through their days without it. It is seldom that people even realize this about themselves. I have even read that some people's adrenal glands are irregular in size due to overuse.

Adrenaline addiction can manifest in ways such as overcommitment, being too busy, inadequate rest and sleep, being easily distracted, inability to sit still or relax, always being in a hurry, rudeness, never feeling like you've accomplished enough. By the way, what is "enough"?

If a person isn't always doing something, then it appears to others that they are wasting time. Have you ever heard someone say, "Don't you have anything better to do than to just sit there?" Many people have lost the ability to just sit and be. Being pumped up with adrenaline makes that very difficult. And add caffeine addiction on top of that. The toll this takes on the body, especially the heart, is astounding.

Day planners rule our lives and dictate our time. Every day on the calendar is filled in. Instead of just letting children "play", parents feel that they have to enroll them in some organized sport or activity…which then necessitates more going, more scheduling. And at what cost?

I remember one December many years ago when the reality of overdoing and overgoing became apparent to me. There were, as usual, lots of fun and meaningful events going on around town. They were all so good that it just seemed a shame not to partake. I had very efficiently scheduled special things for us to go and do during that month. One day, I took a good look at the calendar and realized that there was something planned on almost every day! When would we just be home and enjoy our time together there…without watching the clock and having to be somewhere at a certain time? Where was the possibility for spontaneity?

It wasn't the quality of the events that was the problem…it was the quantity. I picked up a pen and starting marking things out. I finally decided to choose about two things to do away from home and leave all the other days open. What a difference that made! The season was filled with peace and joy and fun instead of stress and fatigue. I learned to be protective of those open days so as not to let busy-ness slip in and fill them.

In our society, "busy-ness" is considered an admirable trait…especially if we are busy doing "good" things…such as caring for our families or doing the Lord's work. It has also become a convenient excuse for neglecting people. I'm sure you've heard people say, "I meant to call (or write or visit, etc.) but I've just been so busy." I truly believe that people pretty much find time for things that are important to them.

Common courtesy has even taken a back seat to busy-ness. Thank you notes are almost obsolete. If it isn't "urgent", then it just doesn't get attention. The important things have been pushed aside by the urgent things. Our society reflects this and even excuses it. We are paying a price for it, too.

Now what does God say about all this? Does it please Him when His children don't have time for Him? By the way, *doing for* God is not a substitute for *being with* God. Does it please Him when we are not at peace, when we are short with people, when we are always going and doing and going and doing and still feel inadequate?

You may be recognizing yourself about now and thinking, "Well, I just can't sit around all day. I have responsibilities." God knows that and a good look at Proverbs will tell you what He thinks about laziness. We have to go, do, accomplish, work, etc. But He does not desire for us to sacrifice our peace in the process.

Perhaps you are familiar with the story of Martha and Mary in Matthew 10. Jesus came to their home to visit. Martha got upset because Mary was sitting at His Feet listening to Him while she (Martha) was busy (distracted) making preparations. She finally had had enough and complained to Jesus about it. His response to her was one of loving wisdom. He did not tell Martha that her activities were *wrong*. He said that Mary has "chosen what is better". He also pointed out to Martha that she (Martha) was "worried and upset about many things". Some people see this story and label Mary as lazy. That just doesn't add up because God despises laziness and yet He said that Mary has chosen what is better. He does not contradict Himself. He was pointing out that spending time with Him was better than the other activities, which consumed Martha. Notice the fruit of Mary's choice...peace, pleasing Jesus. Martha's choice...worried, upset. And by the time she decided she was going to straighten Jesus and Mary out about this situation, you can probably guess that her face was red and her adrenaline was pumping.

Jesus loved them both but their choices brought different reactions from Him. We are important to Him. He longs for our company. Doing God's work is a good thing. Tending to our responsibilities and duties, which are necessary for life on this earth, is a good thing. Spending time alone with God is the better thing. And the reward of that choice is something we all need...something the Lord provides for us because He cares so much for us...His Peace.

The only way to enjoy and walk in His Peace is to spend time alone with Him regularly. Uh-oh...there's that "t" word. If you feel that you don't have any "extra" to spend with Him, then that's part of the problem. God deserves better than our leftovers. He deserves our first and best. Most likely, if your schedule is that full, then there are things in it that God did not ordain. "But they are *good* things", you may say. Even if that's true, if they are keeping you from spending time with your Father, then those activities are robbing you of His Peace.

God will never assign you to do so many things that you are in a continual state of exhaustion, and where He gets neglected, or both. We all get tired at times, for sure, but to carry fatigue as a constant companion is not God's will. Fatigue can bring on depression, which is usually accompanied by despair and hopelessness. Look at that list. That is not what our Father desires for us.

Perhaps you are a single mother, or a homemaker with several children, or a husband working two jobs to support your family, or a wife and mother who has to work outside the home. If you feel like you're "just trying to make it" each day, you are being robbed of God's Peace. You may be thinking, "Well, I'm doing the best I can." There is no doubt about that. The effort being put forth is not at question here.

I would like to ask something, though. In whose strength are you operating? If it's your own, then you know that it has its limits and many of you are probably running on empty. That's why people turn to their adrenaline as a source of fuel without even realizing it. But as I discussed earlier, adrenaline was not designed for use as a regular fuel and it is dangerous, emotionally and physically, to use it that way. "Then what can I do?" I'm so glad you asked.

I'm not going to show you how to get more organized or how to be more efficient with your time or how to delegate tasks. Those are all good traits but there are a lot of organized, efficient people who are still too busy and don't have peace.

My suggestion is quite simple. In fact, so simple that I hope you won't disregard it. In today's complicated lifestyle, we have a tendency to doubt the simple answers. Please don't do that here. I'm suggesting that you ask God to take your "to do" list and your priorities, and to do some trimming and rearranging. Oh, boy, I can hear the outcry now. "I can't drop any of my activities!" "My kids *have* to be in sports and dance and music and scouts." "So and so is counting on me." "If I don't volunteer, it won't get done." "My church group needs me."

Okay – my turn again.

I now ask you how many of these "must do" activities/responsibilities did God direct you to do? It's getting quiet in here. Good, that means you're thinking…or you've left the room. (I hope not.) Seriously, though, please understand that God is *very* aware of every detail in your life. He is a God of details and for that I am very thankful. He cares about your needs and responsibilities and He doesn't want you to be neglectful. He also wants your companionship and you *need* His.

When you allow God to direct your life, your schedule may still be full, but there will most definitely be quality time with your Father…*and* He will give you *His* strength to accomplish what He has directed you to do. With God, it is possible to have a very full lifestyle or schedule and still maintain His Peace within.

On the other hand, we should not expect Him to give us strength for each day's activities when we refuse to give Him any say over those activities. I personally don't believe that God blesses or strengthens us to do things He has not called us to do. If He did so, He would be contributing to our excessive busy-ness and He would be leading us away from His goal for us, which is to enjoy His Presence and His Peace.

"But what if I don't like what God does with my schedule or my life?" "What if He takes out all the things I enjoy?" If you're really thinking this, then you don't know the true nature of God yet. God is a *good* God! He is not a party pooper. He wants you to live an abundant life. He wants you to *enjoy* your life. You need to start seeing Him that way. Break free from any beliefs that portray God as some grumpy old tyrant who is just waiting for you to mess up so He can let you have it. Or some cruel taskmaster who wants to work you to the bone and then discard you when you can't serve him anymore. I realize I'm using strong language here but there are people who actually do see God in this horribly negative light. He is *not* like that! He *made* you. He knows much better than you or anyone else what will make you happy.

Keep in mind, too, that God always blesses and rewards obedience and faith. If we obey Him by submitting our life's activities to Him and then have faith that "…in all things God works for the good of those who love Him, who have been called according to *His purpose*." (Romans 8:28, italics mine), then He will bless us.

I know it is very difficult for most of us to relinquish control…of anything. But let me ask you this. Is your being in control of your life bringing you peace? If not, then you have a wonderful opportunity to change that. Give Him a chance. His plans for you are so much greater than your own plans. And one of His desires for you is to walk in and enjoy His Peace.

Wisdom and Guidance

Wisdom…we can all use more of that. And we need to seek it diligently. The world would tell us to use our own judgement and to do what seems right to us. So, if it seems right for you to steal or to assault someone, then that makes it okay? Not quite. God says in Proverbs 3:5 that we are not to lean on our own understanding, but that we are to trust Him. Proverbs 28:26 tells us that, "He who trusts in himself is a fool, but he who walks in wisdom is kept safe."

The term "fool" as used in the Old Testament comes from the Hebrew word meaning "one who is morally deficient". God knows that if people are left to their own devices and do not govern their lives based on His Wisdom and His Truth, then chaos, confusion, and calamity would be the result. It sounds like our society, doesn't it? So many have turned their backs on God and His Word, and we, as a people, are suffering greatly because of it.

Proverbs 4:7 reads, "Wisdom is supreme; therefore get wisdom..." How do we get wisdom? The world tells us that *experience* is the best teacher. But this is not what God says. Yes, experience can be *a* teacher, but God desires that we learn and gain wisdom without having to go through the painful consequences of unwise choices. Yes we can and do learn from unpleasant experiences, but that is not God's best for us. What kind of Father would He be if He desired for His children to only learn from tragedy, heartache, and failure?

If you, as a parent, tell your child not to touch the fire, then you are imparting wisdom to that child. It is your desire that he will take your advice and *not* touch the fire and, therefore, avoid being burned. He, however, may choose to ignore your warning and put his hand into the fire anyway. The result? He gets burned and definitely learns not to touch fire. *But* was that your *will* that he learn *that* way...through the painful experience? Of course not! It's the same with God. He much prefers that we grow in wisdom and avoid the pitfalls of life so we don't have to suffer the consequences of those pitfalls.

Learning from bad experiences and unwise choices *is* a good way to learn when it's *someone else's* experiences. In 1 Corinthians 10, Paul lists several mistakes that the people of Israel made and also tells us the awful consequences of each. He also points out that God intends for us to use these things as *examples*.

1 Corinthians 10:6 – "Now these things occurred as examples to keep us from setting our hearts on evil things as they did."

1 Corinthians 10:11 – "These things happened to them as examples and were written down as warnings for us…"

As you can see, Paul used the word "examples" twice…to make it clear that we were to learn from *their* mistakes.

I'd like to point out that when we go through bad experiences due to our *own* unwise decisions, and then we learn from that, God can certainly use us to help teach others. He often does. Powerful testimonies can come forth from such experience. His Grace is so amazing! But it is still not His choice for us to learn the painful way.

It is not necessary to have to "experience" something bad in order to teach others about it. I remember an incident in high school, which exemplifies this point. A medical doctor came to speak to us about drugs. Some boy asked, "How can you tell us how bad drugs are for us when you haven't used them?" I have always remembered the doctor's response to that foolish question. He replied, "I don't have to have a heart attack to know that it hurts." What simple wisdom! He sure impressed me with that statement.

The first and best way to get wisdom is in God's Word. 2 Timothy 3:16 reads, "All Scripture is God-breathed and is useful for teaching, rebuking, correcting, and training in righteousness…" The book of Proverbs alone contains a treasure chest of wisdom. One method I have found helpful is to read one chapter of Proverbs each day with the chapter number corresponding with the day of the month. This monthly repetition keeps your mind bathed in wisdom.

In Psalm 111:10 God says that the fear of the Lord is the *beginning* of wisdom. Solomon states, in the first chapter of Proverbs, that fear of the Lord is the beginning of knowledge. All who follow His precepts have good understanding. To fear God means to have deep respect for, awe, and reverence for Him because of Who He is. Only a fool does not reverence God. A fool has no wisdom in him. In the book of Proverbs, you will see wisdom and folly contrasted frequently. You will also see the consequences of each.

Another way to gain wisdom is to listen to and learn from others who value wisdom and knowledge, and are constantly in pursuit of more. Proverbs 13:20 reads, "He who walks with the wise grows wise." How can you know who is wise? Daniel 12:3 tells us that. "Those who are wise will shine like the brightness of the heavens…" You will recognize them when you see them.

You can also ask God for wisdom. In James 1:5 He says, "If any of you lacks wisdom, he should ask God, Who gives generously to all without finding fault, and it will be given to him." Notice He said He gives *generously* to all without finding fault. Perhaps you have asked people for advice or help and you have heard, "I can't believe you don't know that." Or, "I don't have time to teach you…go learn it for yourself like I did." But God doesn't say that to us. He desires for us to have wisdom more than we even desire it.

Hosea 4:6 states, "…my people are destroyed from lack of knowledge." He is saying that what we don't know *can* hurt us. So, go ahead and ask Him.

Psalm 25:9 – "He guides the humble in what is right and teaches them His Way."

Psalm 73:24 – "You guide me with your counsel…"

Psalm 119:130 – "The unfolding of Your Words gives light; it gives understanding to the simple."

Psalm 119:105 – "Your Word is a lamp to my feet and a light for my path."

2 Samuel 22:29 – "You are my lamp, O Lord; the Lord turns my darkness into light."

It is important to understand that when we are seeking God for direction and guidance, that He usually gives us enough "light" for our next step…not our entire journey. Oh, how we long to know more right now. But God knows that if we were told ahead of time what is down the road or around that corner, we probably wouldn't take another step. In His Wisdom, He shows us what we need to know for now.

Years ago, I heard someone refer to this as "flashlight faith". Enough light to see your next step and then trust God to show you the steps after that when you get there. If He showed us the entire road ahead, it would require no trust or faith on our part. The basis of our relationship with God is trusting Him and having faith in His Wisdom to guide us.

God has many names. Names are important to Him. Names are not just a method of identification...they are a definition of a person's character and attributes and purpose in life. That is why He changed several people's names. Abram became Abraham, Sarai became Sarah. He changed Jacob's name to Israel. Simon Bar Jonah was renamed Peter. Saul, after his Damascus Road experience, was known as Paul. When He changed their lives or set them on a path He had created for them, He changed their names so that their identity would be in His Plan doing His Will.

As I said before, God has many names. Why? Because He has so many characteristics and there are so many facets to Him that it takes many names just to attempt to describe Him! Oh, He is such a good and great God! May we never lose sight of just how blessed we are to have the privilege of being called "children of God". (1 John 3:1)

In Isaiah 9:6 He is called "Wonderful Counselor". And yet when we are hurting or need advice or direction, many times He is the last person we turn to. We call everyone else looking for an answer or some comfort, when all the while God is just waiting and wanting us to call Him. By the way, His phone number is Jeremiah 33:3. "Call on Me and I will answer you…"

Notice the differences in the world's answers to your problems and then what God has to say about you…

The world says to "cope" and provides some methods of doing so…but God says to "overcome" and shows you the *One* Way of doing so. The world says to "just get by"…but God says to "thrive". The world says to "survive"…but God says that we are "more than conquerors through Christ."

I like God's advice much better…how about you?

God can and does speak to us through others frequently. But what we hear from others should mostly be confirmation of what God has already spoken to us through His Word or into our spirit. There is such peace in that.

Another of His Names is "Mighty God" in Isaiah 9:6. What a privilege to have a Friend and Counselor Who is always available and Who is the Most Powerful One! When people ask me why or how something good happened, I sometimes like to respond with "I have friends in High Places." And we do! Think about this for a moment…

Wonderful Counselor

Mighty God

And He wants to be your Best Friend

Wow!

God does reveal to us at times a plan He has for us in the future, as He did for Joseph in Genesis. But He usually doesn't tell us *how* it will come to be or when. He can give us a vision or dream and then we have to trust Him with the details, and obey Him step by step. Isaiah 30:21 states, "…your ears will hear a voice behind you, saying, This is the way; walk in it." He will provide the guidance and direction that we need. And we will hear Him if we listen.

One way we recognize someone is by their voice. God's Voice is most likely not going to be audible. You will hear It in your spirit. In order to recognize His Voice, you have to spend time with

Him and have a close relationship with Him. In John 10, Jesus says His sheep follow Him because they know His Voice. The more closely we walk with Him, the easier it will be for us to know when it is God speaking to us and when it is the voice of a "stranger".

We can have wisdom and direction and God desires that for us. We must seek it in His Word, learn from others who possess wisdom and knowledge, ask God for it and believe that He will give it to us, and then listen for His Voice in our spirit.

Even if you have shunned God and His Wisdom in the past and are perhaps thinking it's too late to ask for it now…please know that it is never too late as far as your Father is concerned. You are valuable to Him. You matter to Him. He is a gracious God. He is a forgiving God. He loves you. He is compassionate and His mercies are new *every* morning (Lamentations 3:22-23). I'm so glad!

No matter what you've done in the past, He will give you His Wisdom when you ask for it…and He won't do it begrudgingly. Have you ever made a mistake and then asked someone to teach you a better way? And then they reply with "Okay…" But it's peppered with, "If you had listened to me before…" or "Okay, but you don't really deserve this." "Maybe you'll get it right *this* time." Those statements are loaded with guilt and condemnation, and are intended to make you feel worthless.

But God doesn't say that. He says, "Come with Me. I'd love to show you a better way." "But God, I really messed up." He says, "Today is a *new* day." Aren't you glad He is a God of second chances? and more!

We don't have to wander through life aimlessly. He has given us a road map. But what about detours we take or missed road signs or getting completely off the map…and winding up in a "state" where we don't belong?

Don't worry…

God allows U-turns.

Trust

Trust…what comes to mind when you hear that word? Perhaps warm, loving thoughts, or maybe a painful memory. Does it make you feel comfortable and safe or did you stiffen up a bit? You may even experience a mixture of feelings depending on who came to your mind.

For many of us, trust is an area which presents a challenge. The first thing I want to say here is that God is not the author of anything that has ever happened to you in your life which caused a trust to be broken, or which caused your ability to trust to be weakened. God does not create or orchestrate situations in our lives which cause us to be the *opposite* of what He desires in us and requires of us…that we trust Him.

We all come into this world with a trust level at the top of the scale. It doesn't take effort to trust people…we just do. We have a clean slate and we trust because we've never been given a reason not to. Then time passes and trusts are broken and our trust level begins to wane. With most people, the level is never at its peak again, but sadly, continues to decline with age and experiences. The decline may happen gradually or it may take a severe plunge caused by events such as rejection from a parent, death of a parent, abandonment, molestation by a trusted person, etc.

Did you ever play the game where you close your eyes and fall backwards and trust someone to catch you? It's fun as long as they *catch* you. Perhaps you decided to play, and fell backwards and the person you put your trust in let you fall very painfully to the ground. They even laughed and called it a "joke". Your tailbone probably hurt for a few days but your trust level was affected for longer than that.

As we become adults, the broken trusts come in other forms. The spouse who vowed to love and cherish us has changed their mind and announces that they need a divorce. The wife who promised faithfulness has now decided that her husband doesn't satisfy her anymore and she has found someone who does. The business partner who emptied the vault and left town. The person you confided in about a personal problem you were having has shared that information with others. The husband, whose place it is to protect his wife, has decided to use her as a punching bag. The friend you trusted "borrowed" your credit card or ran up your phone bill and has left you holding the bag. The wife who tells you she is not fulfilled anymore as a homemaker and that she is leaving you and the children so she can go discover herself. You come to a loved one's defense who is accused of something. You put your reputation on the line for them, only to discover that the accusations were valid, and they let you believe otherwise. And then there is no remorse for the damage caused. If you don't see yourself in one of these scenarios, you probably have a few of your own.

The ultimate result of any of these is usually a decline in our trust level...sometimes so severely that we may even make a vow that we will never trust anyone again. What we don't realize is that "anyone" includes God. And that makes sense because if you can't trust those you *can* see, then how can you trust Someone you *can't* see? And yet God expects this of us.

I sense God is prompting me to say something here before I continue on with this chapter. If you are thinking, "How or why should I trust a God Who stood by and did nothing while (you fill in the blank) was happening to me? Where was He then? Why didn't He stop it? Why should I trust Him now?"

First, God was right there when bad or hurtful things were happening to you. He didn't stop it because if He prevented all wrong things from happening in this world, He would be violating His sovereign decision to give humans a free will. He knew when He created us from the very beginning, that there would be those who would choose evil instead of good. They would choose death over life. They would choose not to follow Christ. And yet He *still* gave us free choice, which means those who betrayed you or hurt you were exercising their free will at your expense. If it appears that they got away with their actions, they didn't. They most certainly will be held accountable. But that is not our job. We are to leave that to God. He says that vengeance is His and He will repay. (Deuteronomy 32:35) This doesn't mean that we should not do our part to see that certain individuals in our society who hurt others are put behind bars. Sometimes, that is necessary. But beyond that, God will deal with it. We need to trust in that.

Back to your questions…God was with you then and He is with you now. It was *not* His will that those things happened to you. Talk about false accusations…imagine how the Lord must feel when He is given "credit" for such things as assaults, auto accidents, murder, rape, incest, killer storms, plane crashes, disease, death, fatal illnesses, etc. etc. Who could ever love or trust a God who "brings these things into our lives to teach us something?" I can feel my temperature rising as I write this! Our God is a master at taking *bad* situations, tragedy, piles of garbage, even ashes, and *bringing good out of it.* It takes a loving and powerful Father to be able to do that. And yet instead of just getting glory for the good He brings after the bad, He gets accused of the bad, too.

There is no telling how many people have turned their back on God because they were told that God had caused the tragedy in their life. Try expecting a child to understand why God "took" his mother because He needed her more. No wonder that child grows up with a distorted view of God! As you can see, I don't sit by quietly when my Father is falsely accused.

Okay, let's return now to our discussion. God does expect us to trust Him even though we have experienced betrayals of trust with people. God says in Numbers 23:19 that He doesn't lie and He doesn't change His mind. His Word and His promises to us are true forever. There is no small print or expiration date or loopholes or escape clauses in the covenant (contract) He made with us. I realize that this is a concept which is extremely difficult to comprehend, especially by those who have been betrayed somehow (which includes everyone). However, it still holds true whether we choose to believe it or not.

You don't need to try to tell God all the reasons you cannot trust Him...He was there, remember? It broke His Heart to see your trust betrayed. He also knew He would be the One left standing with you to pick up the pieces, because He loves you and He wants your trust. And He should have it because He is most certainly worthy of it!

Trusting God, like so many other facets of our relationship with Him, is a process…a lifelong process…and we are to continually be moving to a higher level of trust in Him. When we submit to Him, and express our desire to trust him more and more, His Heart is touched by this. He is a God of restoration and longs to restore our trust level that was damaged by others and by circumstances. He lovingly places us in situations where we must trust Him because there is no other way.

During these times of growth, you may be tempted to think, "God, where are You? I thought you said I could trust You." He delights in proving Himself faithful and true and at just the right time, He comes through for us like a Knight in shining armor. And what is the effect on our trust level with Him? It goes up a notch or two. Then He is able to work in our lives and through us because He knows we are trusting Him more.

I used to have a poster which showed a girl happily swinging on a swing with a big smile or her face. She was leaning way back so she could swing higher and higher. The ropes of the swing were suspended from and were being completely supported by one thing…God's finger. The caption read, "Do you trust Me?" That poster spoke volumes!

It would be wrong for me to say that trusting God will always be easy. It can be most challenging at times, but the rewards and benefits are well worth it. Imagine how you would feel if your little child didn't trust that you would be there for him in the morning when he woke up. You've *always* been there, you've *never* given him a reason to think otherwise. And yet he doubts your word. Without cause, he doesn't trust you. Pretty frustrating, huh? And hurtful...

Well, imagine the Heavenly Father's heartbreak when His children don't trust Him. And yet He continues to reach out to us and looks for opportunities to show His faithfulness. He is a very patient and gentle Father. How thankful I am for that!

Remember what I said earlier in this chapter about how as young children we trust so freely and easily? Well, *we* are *God's* children...no matter our age...and He says we are to trust Him. He means it. And after all, *He* has never given us a reason not to.

I stated at the beginning of this chapter that trust is a challenge for many of us. I sense that there are many of you reading this who have found this chapter to be a difficult one. So, please allow me to speak directly to you...

I would like to say to you that I am so very sorry for anything that anyone ever did to you that betrayed your trust. I also am sorry about anything that happened in your life to cause you to withdraw from God. I know that your pain is very real, and that time alone does *not* heal.

Please take a step...even a baby step...toward allowing the Lord to touch those areas that still hurt. He knows about every one of them...and it hurts Him, too. You see, He knows how it feels to be betrayed. He loves you so very much and you are so precious to Him.

Please take that first step toward Him. He is longing to show you that He alone can heal those hurts and that He is trustworthy.

He is right there with you, precious one...waiting with outstretched Arms...for *you.*

Protection

One of the responsibilities of a father is to protect his children. Many of you reading this were not protected by your father. Either he was not around due to death, divorce or some other reason. Perhaps he was there but he was negligent. Sadly, there are some who actually needed protection *from* their father. How like satan to take God's plan and then twist and pervert it to the point that the one designated as protector becomes a source of abuse.

In any case, if you were not protected properly as a child by your earthly father, then it becomes difficult to expect or even believe that you will be protected by your Heavenly Father. So you built walls around yourself. You may have adopted the creed that, "I can't depend on anyone to protect me so I'm going to just protect myself." Or you may have been told that you better watch out for yourself because you can't count on anyone else to do it. Just take care of number one. But that's not what God says. In Proverbs 2:8, He says

He guards and protects His faithful ones. In Psalm 121 the phrase "He watches over" is repeated five times even though there are only eight verses total. When God repeats things, He isn't just being redundant. He is doing it to make an important point. He wants to make certain we get the message.

In Psalm 91:14, God says He will rescue and protect us. There are *many* verses in the Bible regarding protection. I have listed a few here.

Psalm 91:11 – "…He will command his angels concerning you to guard you in all your ways."

Proverbs 18:10 – "The Name of the Lord is a strong tower; the righteous run into it and are safe."

Psalm 31:23 – "…the Lord preserves the faithful…"

Psalm 124:6 – "Praise be to the Lord, who has not let us be torn by their teeth."

Psalm 55:18 – "He ransoms me unharmed from the battle waged against me, even though many oppose me."

Perhaps you are thinking that what you need protection from is just too big and nobody can help. Well, your Heavenly Protector has an answer to that, too. Look at Isaiah 59:19. "...When the enemy shall come in like a flood, the Spirit of the Lord shall lift up a standard against him." (KJV) Romans 8:31 says, "...if God is for us, who can be against us?" No matter how big the enemy (or situation) looks or is, God raises His standard of protection to a higher level. Please don't ever believe that satan and God are evenly matched and we just have to hope that God wins. No way! No how! Not ever! Jesus defeated satan 2000 years ago when He came out of the tomb. satan is a defeated foe! Never forget that. You may ask, "Then why is he still causing so much trouble?" Because he is a poor loser and because he knows Bible prophecy better than you or I do. He knows his days are numbered and he also knows his final destination. He's not going out without a fight. So, you must remember whose side you're on. As a child of God, you are on the side of the Champion...Jesus Christ! Hallelujah!

Jeremiah 39:17-18 says "...I will rescue you on that day, declares the Lord; you will not be handed over to those you fear...I will save you;...*because* you trust in Me, declares the Lord." (italics mine) Notice that last phrase...because you trust in Me. There is a tendency to overlook that part or not place much importance on those words. God does not waste words nor are any of His Words

107

meaningless. He included that to show that we have a responsibility in this relationship, too. If you're thinking, "I knew there was a catch," please think about this. Any healthy relationship is a two way street, with both parties giving and both receiving. What kind of relationship is it where one person does everything? A pretty lopsided one, for sure.

What God requires of us is that we trust Him and obey Him. When we do that, then He promises to protect us. If you search the Scriptures for verses regarding God's protection, you will find many. Praise God! You will also almost always find a reference as to what our responsibility is.

Some people attempt to use God's promise to protect us in ways it was never intended. Such as driving carelessly or way too fast for no reason, taking silly chances with your life, doing things on a dare, going to a place or event where you *know* you don't belong, sexual promiscuity, leaving all your doors unlocked or open at night...the list goes on. God gave us intelligence and I believe He expects us to use it.

All of us have done foolish things or we've done things that are just plain wrong. Sometimes, we have had to suffer the consequences and other times it seems we haven't. The latter can mistakenly lead us to think that we just "got away with it" or that God protected us anyway. And then that line of thinking can lead us to actually doing it again.

It is important to understand that it is God's mercy alone that protected us, or God honoring the prayers of others on our behalf, even when we were out of His will, or in disobedience to Him. We don't get away with things. But He is such a merciful Father that His protection sometimes reaches beyond the lines He has set for us. Keep in mind that when we step out from under God's umbrella of protection, then He is *not* obligated to protect us.

If it's raining, and your child refuses to stand under your umbrella, he is going to get wet. You may decide to let that happen, or you may, out of your love for him, go to *where he is and cover him.* But what does the latter teach him? He learns that, yes, you do love and care about him. *But* he also learns that he can be disobedient and still be protected.

If God always provided protection for us in our disobedience, He would be contributing to our rebellion. He is not going to do that. We have all stretched His mercy, for sure. But if He senses that we will not turn around and get on the right path, He has no choice but to withdraw His protection. Unfortunately, at that point, when circumstances turn ugly, God then gets blamed for it. He is no more responsible for those circumstances than a parent is responsible for a child getting wet when they refuse to stay under the umbrella. That parent didn't call rain down on the child! The child's *choice to disobey* is what got him wet.

When we truly grasp just how great our Father's grace and mercy are, we can't help but fall to our knees and thank Him and thank Him and thank Him for His kindness and His protection...especially when we didn't deserve it.

Only a fool attempts to toy with Almighty God. And the "master of folly" did just that. In Matthew 4, one of the ways satan tempted Jesus was to take Him to the highest point of the temple and then tell him to jump! Then he had the audacity to quote Scripture! Keep in mind that satan had already tempted Jesus another way and Jesus' response was Scripture. I guess he figured that if *he* (satan) used Scripture then Jesus would be impressed and would go along with it. he used verses from Psalm 91 regarding angels lifting Him up and protecting Him. What a fool! He actually thought he could trick Jesus into "proving" God's promise of protection by leaping off that temple. Well, Jesus' reply is so good! satan's attempt to distort and misuse the Word was met with more *Word*. I love this. Jesus, the "Living Word", the "Word Made Flesh", is quoting the "Written Word". (John 1:1) satan is being hit with both barrels. Jesus said, "It is *also* written, do not put the Lord your God to the test." My own translation goes something like this..."satan, I'm well aware that you are quoting Psalm 91, and I'm also aware that you are misusing it. Don't you realize Who you are dealing with here? **I AM** the Word!"

The point of all this is that we are not to tempt God by purposely doing something we know to be wrong and then expect Him to protect us again and again, just because He did it before. Oh yes, God is most definitely a God of mercy and grace. In fact, His mercies are new every morning. (Lamentations 3:23) Oh, how I am thankful for that! But a wise and grateful person does not push the envelope. In Romans 6:1-2 we can see Paul's emphasis regarding this point. "...Shall we go on sinning so that grace may increase?" By no means!"

So what does God say about you regarding protection?

"I love you."

"You are my child. I don't want you harmed."

"I promise to protect you."

"Stay close to Me so I can do so."

On another note, some of you may be thinking that you have trusted God and obeyed Him and are serving Him with all your heart and yet something bad still happened to you. Perhaps a car wreck or you were assaulted or you were falsely accused or your house burned. "Where was God then?" "Why didn't He protect me then?"

I doubt I can answer those questions to your complete satisfaction but I'd like you to think about something. Are you aware of *all* the times God protected you? I don't think so. A traffic light, a long line at the store...things none of us regard as "protection devices". But it may just be that God used these very annoyances to keep you from a dangerous situation. I've experienced this many times.

Perhaps you've had a "hunch" about something or someone, and you followed that feeling and then later you discovered that you were spared some kind of danger or loss. Well, that "hunch" or "gut feeling" was God warning you and protecting you.

Are your children aware of *every* thing you protected them from throughout their growing up years? Of course not. There are so many times you protected them emotionally as well as physically, that they know nothing about. Well, it's the same with our Father, but much more so.

Instead of questioning Him about the bad things we *know* about, let's focus on thanking Him for the protection He provided that we *do* know about as well as the millions of times He has protected us that we *don't* know about.

Imagine your children saying to you, "Mom, Dad, I want to thank you for protecting me from that dangerous situation we just went through. And I also want to thank you for all the times throughout my life that you have protected me, including the times that I'm not even aware of. I realize that I would not be where I am today without your watchful, loving eye over me and your continual intervention on my behalf." Wow! Talk about feeling appreciated! What parent wouldn't desire to hear this kind of gratitude?

To say that God does a mighty fine job of protecting His children is an understatement, for sure. He adores a thankful heart. Let's remember to thank Him. After all, He is a Parent and He has feelings, too.

Thank you, Father.

Fear and Worry

Fear. It's something most people live with on a daily basis. And it's also considered normal and acceptable. Our society has even taken the word "phobia" and attached it to a myriad of words. Somehow, if we can place a label on our fears then that makes them at least "manageable".

But that is not what God says about fear. He never told us to label or manage fear. Throughout His Word, we are told to "fear not". Then why are we told to fear the Lord? When God says we are to fear Him, that is not referring to being afraid of Him or walking on pins and needles around Him. To fear the Lord means to reverence Him, to stand in awe of Him, to have high regard and deep respect for Him. There is a difference in reverencing someone and being afraid of them.

Regarding everything else, we are told repeatedly to not be afraid. Does this mean we are to walk about foolishly as if we are invincible? Of course not. God expects us to use common sense and He also wants us to trust Him and to know that He is always with us. When we learn to rely on Him for our lives and for the circumstances around us, it brings peace into our hearts and minds and bodies. When we are walking in peace instead of fear, we function better, we make wiser decisions, we are more efficient with our time, and we are certainly healthier.

We are also told in Matthew 6 *not* to worry. Jesus didn't say "try" not to worry. He said do *not* worry. He also says in John 14:27, "...Do not let your hearts be troubled and do not be afraid." Worry and fear are in the same family and almost always accompany each other. They create the same negative effects in our minds and have the same detrimental effects on our physical health. This is why we are admonished to not walk in fear and worry. There is absolutely no good that comes out of either.

You may say, "I've always had a fear of this or that and I can't help it." Or "I've always been a worrier, so was my mother and it just runs in my family." "How can I call myself a good parent or spouse, etc., if I don't worry?" At this point you have to make a choice. It doesn't matter how long or why you have feared or worried. God wants us to trust Him and also obey Him. By refusing to turn from fear and worry, you are choosing to disobey and distrust God. As a child of God, I know you do not desire to intentionally do either. You must decide that you are going to walk on a new path. "Well, how do I do that?" I was hoping you'd ask.

No matter how many years or decades you have been in the rut of fear and worry it *is* possible to take a higher road. Remember, a rut is just a grave with the ends kicked out. Get out of that rut by saying *what God says about you* regarding this. Each and every time fear and worry come knocking...and they will...respond with God's Word. There are many verses about fear in the Bible. Do your own search and write them down and keep them at your fingertips. If you say them enough, they will become embedded in your heart and they will become a part of who you are and how you see yourself.

If you say God's Word and believe it with your heart long enough, there will come a time when you are confronted with worry or fear and automatically you will speak or think God's Word. It may even surprise you at first when that happens! Rejoice and be thankful that His Word has been written in your heart. I heard the following saying long ago and I love it. "Fear knocked at my door. When faith went to answer it, nobody was there." Yessss!

If you're wondering how long this transition will take, there is not a blanket answer. A lot of it depends on you and your commitment and determination to living free from this pair of parasites. Also remember Who is helping you along the way.

Think of a large ship that is moving in one direction at a good rate of speed. Then the captain decides that a change of course is needed and orders it. At that point, the rudder is moved which starts the ship on a new course. But a huge ocean liner cannot turn on a dime. It takes a while to turn it, but as long as the rudder is "on course", the ship will eventually follow suit and be on its *new* course.

You are the captain of your ship (your thoughts). You saying and believing God's Word in the midst of fear and worry is your rudder. Hold fast, Captain, and know that the Lord is aboard, helping you and strengthening you. The view should start improving soon!

One last word. Be determined in this fantastic transition you are making in your identity. Remember you have an enemy who is the author of fear and worry. He wants to keep you captive to this, and he is not going to walk away without a fight. But remember that you have the Greater One residing in you. (1 John 4:4) With God's help, you will have the victory!

Also, be patient with yourself. Keep your hands on the wheel so you don't slip back into the old groove. But, if you do slip, don't chastise yourself. Just acknowledge what has happened. You just slipped. See it for what it is...a temporary set back...and then get back on the "high road". Use *both* hands, if necessary! In time your new path will create its own groove and it will be where you tread on a regular basis.

Shame & Disgrace
Guilt & Condemnation

Have you ever had any of these kinds of thoughts?

- "I'm the only one who feels this way."

- "Nobody else does this."

- "I'm the only one this has happened to."

- "I can't tell anyone because nobody would understand."

- "I must be the only one going through this."

These types of thoughts can and often do lead to shame and disgrace about one's self. Shame and disgrace are prison walls that are *not* erected by your Heavenly Father and He does not want you there.

In case you don't already know this, you are most certainly *not* the only one going through anything. Those types of thoughts are not coming from God. If other people have said to you that you are strange to feel that way or that nobody else feels the way you do – well those statements aren't from God either. The important thing is what God *does* say about this. There are many verses in His Word that state that His people will not be put to shame or disgraced.

Isaiah 50:7 reads, "Because the Sovereign Lord helps me, I will not be disgraced. Therefore have I set my face like flint, and I know I will not be put to shame." Setting your face like flint means having a firm, determined belief that this is so...that since the Sovereign Lord is helping you, disgrace and shame do *not* have a place in you!

Joel 2:27 tells us, "...I am the Lord your God and that there is none other...never again will my people be shamed." When we understand that God is the *only* true God, that there is none other, and that He is *our* God, we can claim His promises that we will never be shamed.

Psalm 34:5 says, "Those who look to Him are radiant; their faces are never covered with shame." The key here is "those who look to *Him*". When we do this, He says our faces are radiant. When Moses left the mountain top after spending time in God's presence, his face was radiant. It was bright and glowing. When we look to God and not to ourselves or others, we will not be ashamed but we will reflect the love He feels for us. And just as the people noticed Moses' face, people will see it in yours, too.

It is important to understand that there is a difference in how God views our behavior/actions and our value to Him as His child. God hates sin but still loves the sinner. There are times when we *should* be ashamed of something we've done. But we are not to be ashamed of who we are. God will speak to us in our hearts regarding it, just like parents speak to children about something they have done that needs to be corrected. What we hear from Him, though, will be *conviction* not condemnation. There is a big difference. If the message you hear is filled with accusations, put-downs, reminders of previous mistakes, hopelessness, etc., you must know that that is not conviction from God. It is condemnation from satan. You need to recognize it right away for what it is and reject it in the power of Jesus' Name.

When God is convicting you about something, you will feel remorse over it but you will not feel worthless because of it. Also, you will have a desire to do what is needed to correct it. Ask God's forgiveness and accept His forgiveness, then do whatever He prompts you to do regarding another person you may have hurt, any damage you may have caused, etc.

After this, you are to let it go and move forward. God will not throw it in your face. Others might…satan will…but God won't. And what *God* says about you is what really matters, right?

Jesus kept company with sinful men and women not because He approved of their *ways*…He didn't…but because He loved *them* and desired to see them turn from their ways and follow Him. He valued them and His Love for them poured forth from His Being. When they saw this and realized that they mattered to Him, they viewed themselves differently. Thus, their actions followed suit because their desires were changed due to their relationship with Jesus.

Many times it is our lack of self worth that is the motivational force behind our undesirable traits and behaviors. That lack of value for ourself usually stems from a major traumatic event or a series of emotional, verbal, or physical mistreatment by others. It plays out like this:

Mistreatment Or Abuse or Trauma	>	Little or no sense of self worth	>	Undesirable behavior and attitudes

As humans, we act out of what we believe about ourselves. Up to this point, most, if not all, of what we believe about ourselves came from the opinions of others. God understands *why* we are the way we are but He loves us too much to allow us to stay that way. He is a God of redemption. Hallelujah! His Word is more powerful than *all* the words you have heard and believed for a lifetime.

Think of His Word, His opinion of you, not as a marker to cover over the wrong thinking, but rather as a giant "eraser". He desires to remove the old thoughts and replace them with what He says about you. We must *unlearn* anything we have believed that is contrary to what God says about us...no matter how long we have believed it and no matter who taught us those beliefs. We must learn what our Heavenly Father says about us.

If you have ever felt, for any reason, that you are "damaged goods", I want you to hear this LOUD AND CLEAR. That is a lie!

Our Father *never* sees His children as damaged goods so we should not view ourselves that way either.

Perhaps you are divorced, you were raped, you were abandoned by a parent(s), you didn't graduate high school, you had an abortion, you were molested as a child, you were born out of wedlock or had a baby out of wedlock, you have a speech impediment (by the way, Moses did, too). You've spent time in prison, you were never elected for anything, or won any awards…the list is endless. But you get the picture. *No matter what you have done or what has been done to you, you are not damaged goods!*

If you think that God can never use you and wouldn't even want to because of your past…hear this again, LOUD AND CLEAR. That, too, is a lie. On the contrary, God takes people who satan or the world had labeled as losers or inferior, and He uses them in mighty ways. Those who have "been through stuff" are actually better suited to minister to others in certain situations. Why? Because they've been there and they can now share with other people how Jesus brought them from *where they were to where they are*. As a result, people are set free and are able to live better and happier lives *and* God gets the glory!

What a deal!

Maintaining Your Identity

(Handling the Bumps Along the Way)

Understanding our identity in Christ is a lifelong process. Sometimes we move forward on the path in giant leaps and sometimes we gain this knowledge step by step. What's important is that we "stay the course", remain on the path, and avoid detours and distractions.

If this is all new to you, then I'm sure you are experiencing joy and excitement and a new sense of freedom. I am so thrilled for you! I would be negligent, however, if I didn't give you proper warning and preparation for some bumps or potholes which lay ahead. As a child of God, you have an enemy – satan – who is not pleased with the journey you are now on. He will try his best to trip you up in any way he can. His desire is to knock or lure you off this path.

Stand firm and do not allow him to do this to you. You may be asking, "How do I do that?" One way is the "stop and replace" method. Whenever you hear in your mind or from others the "old tapes", recognize those words and thoughts for what they are…a lie. Do not listen, do not argue, and do not accept those lies. Immediately say "no" (depending on where you are, either whisper it or say it out loud) but you need to be able to hear your words with your own ears. Then *speak* what God says about you regarding this issue or area. Why is it important to *say* words and not just think them? Romans 10:17 states, "…faith comes for *hearing* the message, and the message is heard through the Word of Christ." Say it with force, if necessary. Remember that you have an enemy and you are in a battle – the battlefield being your mind. You must say it like you mean it even if it seems strange to you. If you are thinking, "How can I say it like I mean it, when I'm not sure I believe it yet?" Don't worry, just do it. Do it in faith. After a while of this, you *will* come to believe what God says about you. The old tapes will become strange to you and you will reject those thoughts and they will lose their power over you and their hold on your mind.

Another reason you need to *speak* what God says about you is because there is power in the tongue…in the spoken word. God *spoke* the world into existence. In Genesis 1, the phrase "God said" occurs at least nine times, referring to the creation of the heavens and the earth. God made us in His image or likeness, which means that our words have power, too.

Also, when you *speak* something, your thoughts are interrupted. You *want* to interrupt any wrong thoughts, which are contrary to what God says about you.

Keep in mind that sometimes those closest to us can be used as tools against us. They are not necessarily doing anything knowingly but still can impede our growth and progress on this journey. Sometimes others don't want us to change. They are comfortable with us the way we have been. Perhaps they fear that as we develop our identity in Christ, that we may not want or need them any longer. So they may perceive our growth as a threat. Sometimes, others see us developing and resent it because they realize that they need to make some changes in their life and yet aren't willing to or are afraid to do so. So, instead of confronting themselves, they may confront us. You may hear things such as, "Why are you doing this?" "You're fine the way you are." "Do you *really* think you can change the way you think?" "Who do you think you are?" "What makes you think you're so special?"…and the list goes on.

Remember…and this is important…that people are *not* your enemy…satan is. He can work through people and often does. But you can reject what a person *says* while not rejecting the person. Your battle is with the enemy and the battlefield is your mind. Respond to people with love and yet be firm. Sometimes love must be tough. You might say, "I care about you / I love you but I will not accept what you are saying to me." Say this with kindness but also with strength and conviction. In time, after hearing you respond consistently this way, people will see the positive changes in you and they will either accept you or they won't.

You cannot control others. You can, however, love them without allowing them to impede your growth and your relationship with the Lord. In time, they may come to see and respect the positive changes in you. They may even decide to start this journey themselves. What a joy and a privilege to have your blessings spill over onto other people.

On this journey, it's okay if you slip or even fall down. Just pick yourself up. As long as you are moving forward, then you are making progress. Remember that a huge ship cannot change directions on a dime. It turns gradually, but as long as the rudder is in the correct position, the turn will be definite.

Encourage yourself in the Lord. (1 Samuel 30:6) You can't depend on others to remind you of your value in Christ. The Lord does use others to encourage us this way, for sure, and we are called to edify one another. But, many times when you are hearing the "old messages" and are starting to doubt your value, it will be when you are alone. This is why you must encourage yourself and stand up to the lies and reject them in Jesus' Name.

There are a lot of opinions out there. Most people make the mistake of listening to all of them and then trying to figure out from that conglomeration who they are. Whew! No wonder so many people are confused and unsure about their identity.

However, there is only One opinion that truly matters, that will never waver or change. That is God's opinion of you, which is contained in His Word. Think of His opinion (His Word) as a plumb line. When builders are constructing a house they have to have some kind of accurate gauge in order to determine a *true* vertical line so that the walls of the house will be straight and not leaning. A plumb line is a string with a weight on the end. It is *always* accurate. If the builders just go by how the walls line up to the ground around it, the house will not be straight or sturdy because the ground will most likely *not* be perfectly level.

Now, imagine that your identity is like that house. You want and need to be sturdy and strong. In order to be that way, you have to build your house (your identity) based on a *true* opinion of who you are and your value. Any words or opinions you hear that do not line up with your plumb line (God's opinion) must be discarded as false. No matter how true the words may sound or even feel, or who is saying them, *always* measure them against God's Word. And always choose to speak and believe what **God** says about you.

I would like to leave you with this blessing from 2 Corinthians 13:14:

"May the grace of the Lord Jesus Christ,

and the love of God,

and the fellowship of the Holy Spirit

be with you all."

Amen.

Prayer of Salvation

While writing this book, I knew that some of the readers would not be among those who have a personal relationship with Jesus Christ. The promises and scriptures in this book, which are taken from the Bible, are not for anyone and everyone but they *are* for each and every one of God's children.

In order to be a child of God and to have the privilege and honor of calling Him "Father", a person must come to Him through His Son, Jesus Christ, and be born again. In John 14:6 Jesus says, "...I am the way and the truth and the life. No one comes to the Father except through me."

If you already have that personal relationship with Jesus, then, as God's son or daughter, you can claim every Word as your own.

If you have never taken this most important step and are ready to do so, then I most joyfully congratulate you on your decision! All you need to do is pray this prayer aloud and believe it with your heart. Romans 10:9 says, "That if you confess with your mouth, "Jesus is Lord," and believe in your heart that God raised Him from the dead, you will be saved."

Let's pray…

Dear God, I confess that I am a sinner and need a Savior. I believe that Jesus Christ paid the price for all of my sins by shedding His precious blood and dying on the cross. I believe that you raised Him from the dead. I ask your forgiveness, God, and I want to be your son/daughter. Jesus, please come into my heart and be my Savior and Lord. Thank you. I receive by faith your forgiveness and I know that You now live in me and that I am Yours. In Jesus' Name, Amen.

Congratulations! You are now a child of God!
Welcome to the Family

If you would like to obtain more copies of this book, they are available in bookstores, as well as online via www.amazon.com, www.barnesandnoble.com, etc.

You may also order them directly from the publisher at www.1stbooks.com or by calling them at 888-280-7715.

If you are interested in having the author speak at your meeting, church, or conference, you may contact her at:

Janine Dodds
P.O. Box 645
Taylors, SC 29687

Email – Janine4JC@aol.com

Printed in the United States
46301LVS00005B/166-171

9 781410 770820